The Ultimate Guide to Making Outdoor Gear and Accessories

Books by Monte Burch

The Untimate Guide to Calling and Decoying Waterfowl
Field Dressing and Butchering Deer
Field Dressing and Butchering Upland Birds, Waterfowl, and Wild Turkeys
Field Dressing and Butchering Rabbits, Squirrels, and Other Small Game
Field Dressing and Butchering Big Game
The Field & Stream All-Terrain-Vehicle Handbook
Denny Brauer's Jig Fishing Secrets
Denny Brauer's Winning Tournament Tactics
Black Bass Basics
Guide to Calling & Rattling Whitetail Bucks
Guide to Successful Turkey Calling
Guide to Calling & Decoying Waterfowl
Guide to Successful Predator Calling
Pocket Guide to Seasonal Largemouth Bass Patterns
Pocket Guide to Seasonal Walleye Tactics
Pocket Guide to Old Time Catfish Techniques
Pocket Guide to Field Dressing, Butchering & Cooking Deer
Pocket Guide to Bowhunting Whitetail Deer
Pocket Guide to Spring & Fall Turkey Hunting
Guide to Fishing, Hunting & Camping Truman
The Pro's Guide to Fishing Missouri Lakes
Waterfowling, A Sportsman's Handbook
Modern Waterfowl Hunting
Shotgunner's Guide
Gun Care and Repair
Outdoorsman's Fix-It Book
Outdoorsman's Workshop
Building and Equipping the Garden and Small Farm Workshop
Basic House Wiring
Complete Guide to Building Log Homes
Children's Toys and Furniture
64 Yard and Garden Projects You Can Build
How to Build 50 Classic Furniture Reproductions
Tile Indoors and Out
The Home Cabinetmaker
How to Build Small Barns & Outbuildings
Masonry & Concrete
Pole Building Projects
Building Small Barns, Sheds & Shelters
Home Canning & Preserving (with Joan Burch)
Building Mediterranean Furniture (with Jay Hedden)
Fireplaces (with Robert Jones)
The Homeowner's Complete Manual of Repair and Improvement (with three others)
The Good Earth Almanac Series
Survival Handbook
Old-Time Recipes
Natural Gardening Handbook

The Ultimate Guide to Making Outdoor Gear and Accessories

Complete, Step-by-Step Instructions for Making Decoys, Knives, Gun Stocks, Fishing Lures, Tents, Gun Cabinets, and Much More.

MONTE BURCH

THE LYONS PRESS
Guilford, Connecticut
An imprint of The Globe Pequot Press

10 9 8 7 6 5 4 3 2 1

Library of Congress Cataloging-in-Publication Data is available on file.

Contents

1

Restocking Guns

Guns are a prized possession to many out-doorsmen. When a trusty old gun—whether it be a shotgun, rifle, or pistol—goes by the wayside from a busted or cracked stock, re-stocking it is normally a fairly easy task, even for those without a full shop of woodworking tools.

First, order a replacement stock from a stock-manufacturing company. Make sure that you indicate the proper gun type, model, and stock. Often the difference between two completely different stocks is so little that you might get a stock that appears to fit, but a tiny bit left out of the inletting could make all the difference between an easy job or a frustrat-ing chore.

You can also change the stock and forearm pattern on a gun by ordering a different type. For instance, the narrow forearm grip on some older shotguns can be exchanged for a more easily handled and comfortable beaver-tail forearm. The first step is to remove the old stock. Pay particular attention to the de-tails of how each part comes off the stock—each must come off and go back in its proper sequence, same as on a watch. Place all parts

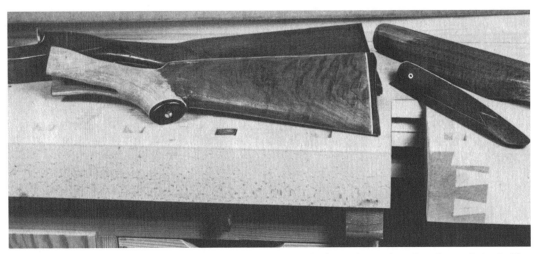

An old, but usable shotgun can often be "recycled" by replacing a busted or deteriorated stock. You can also custom build a gun by changing stock pattern forearm grip.

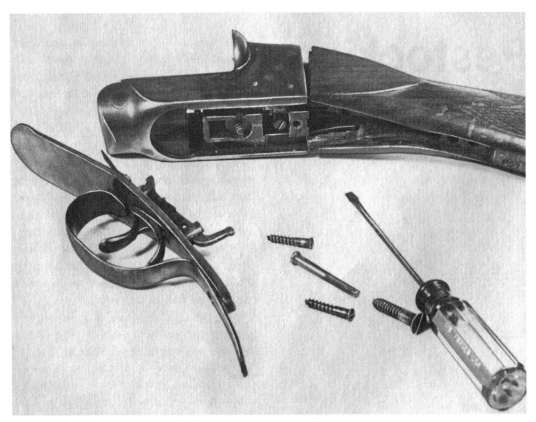

Remove all parts from old gun using the proper size screwdriver.

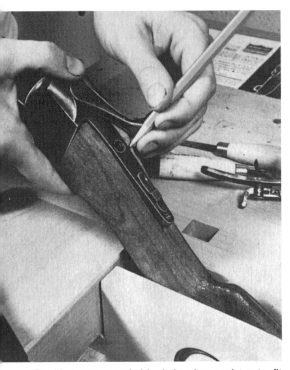

Position new stock blank in vise and try to fit parts in it, marking those areas that need to be cut down.

Metal and wood should blend together with no evidence of a joint. Each surface should match and be flush with the other.

Using small rasps, files, chisels, etc., cut down stock so metal will fit properly.

Coat metal surfaces with light blue chalk and tap into position to mark those areas that cause trouble on the inside of the inletting.

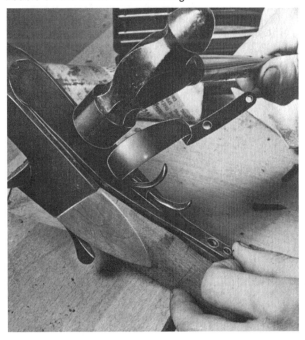

in a pan or a box to ensure that none gets lost in the process. If the gun is particularly tricky, such as on some of the older double-barrel shotguns, it's a good idea to make up a rough drawing of how it comes apart, so when you start putting it back together you won't have any problems getting the various pieces in their proper places.

Place the new semi-inletted stock in position on the gun. You will note that a good deal of wood has to be eliminated in some areas, yet practically none in others. In order to see what needs to be removed from inside the stock, coat the metal pieces that might contact the wood with light blue chalk, then fit the metal into the wood. The areas of wood that will need to be removed will be marked with blue. Wipe off chalk and lightly oil the gun works. Inletting a gunstock is slow, painstaking work. Cut away just a bit of wood at a time, then fit the metal to it. It will take many fittings before the metal and wood pieces fit together properly. Be careful not to cut away too much wood at any one time. If a part and the stock don't match, not only will they look bad, but the gun will be weakened as well.

The inside inletted areas of the stock can be shaped by using tiny woodworking chisels, rasps, and a special rasp called an inletting tool, which is a round-shaped tool that is particularly good for inletting rifle barrels.

When the inside surfaces mate properly, position the parts together and mark for the locations of the screws. Use small drill bits to bore starter holes for the screws, then screw together temporarily. Mark the outside areas that must be shaped, or have wood removed, take the gun apart, and again use rasps and chisels to shape the wood to fit the metal. This also means a lot of fitting and shaping to get a good-looking gun with no depressions or high spots of the wood around the metal. When all this suits satisfactorily, remove the metal parts and shape the rest of the stock to suit.

To ensure that flat portions of stock stay flat, use a wide rasp when shaping these areas.

After boring screw starting holes, temporarily fasten metal to wood to determine fit.

Most stock blanks are about 10 percent larger overall than needed, so you will have plenty of leeway for shaping and sizing the stock to suit. Cut the end of the stock off at the proper angle and fit a recoil pad in place. Hold the pad in place on the stock and mark with an awl through the pad and into the stock for location of the screw holes. Then place the pad and any decorative spacers on the end of the stock and drive screws in through the pad. The pad is also held in place with ordinary white glue. Note that the screws will be driven completely through the recoil pad backing and into the solid portion of the pad, being concealed by the back of the pad. Use the proper size screwdriver so you don't mess up the back of the pad during this operation. With the pad secured to the stock, grind the pad down to match the surrounding surfaces of the stock, using a belt or disk sander.

Use progressively finer grits of sandpaper to get the stock as smooth as possible, then use extra-fine steel wool to put a final satin-smooth surface on it. Tape the recoil pad with masking tape and finish the stock using gunstock-finishing material. This can be a hand-rubbed oil finish or one of the sprayed polyurethane stock finishes. It will take several coats of the finish to get the

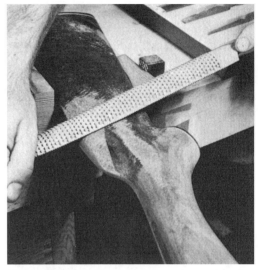

Then rough-shape rest of the stock to suit, using rasps, chisels, etc.

deep look of a properly finished stock and to bring out the color and depth of the wood. Use fine steel wool between coats to achieve the smooth finish. After the last coat, remove the masking tape from the recoil pad and buff the stock to a final satin-smooth finish. Install the metal parts on the gun being careful not to mar the finish on either the wood or the metal.

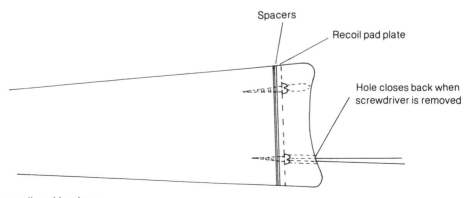

Spacers

Recoil pad plate

Hole closes back when screwdriver is removed

Fasten recoil pad in place.

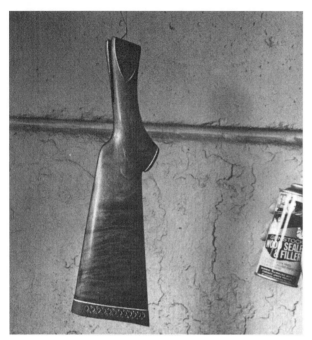

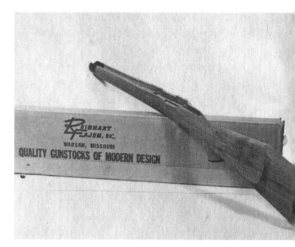

A rifle stock can be replaced in the same manner as the shotgun stock.

Entire stock is sanded smooth with progressively finer grits of sandpaper and finished with a good gunstock finish.

CHECKERING

If you wish to checker the stock, you can do so using purchased tools or you can make up your own. Homemade checkering tools are made of steel bolts or rods ground and filed to the shapes shown. The handles are turned on a lathe and the metal cutting portions glued in the handles with epoxy cement.

A good checkering cradle can take a lot of the frustration and trouble out of the job by holding the stock securely yet allowing you to turn it at any angle to get down in the grooves. Make up the checkering cradle as shown.

Checkering on gunstocks is completely different for each type of stock, but some basic patterns can be used to fit your particular type of gun. Make cardboard templates of the pattern that best fits your gun and place the

Note plastic end grip installed on stock. It is shaped at the same time as the stock is shaped, then all is sanded smooth and finished.

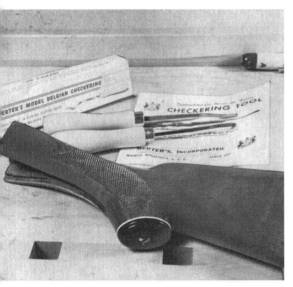

You can do your own checkering using purchased tools.

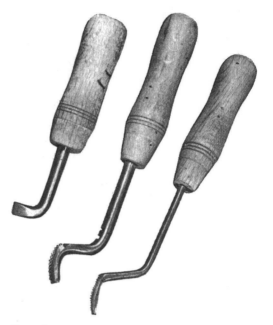

Or make your own.

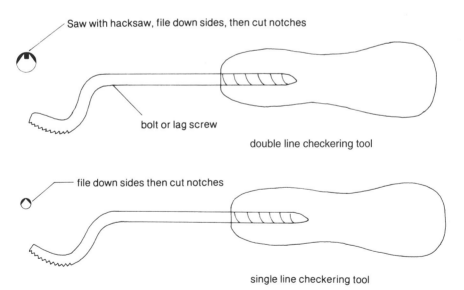

Saw with hacksaw, file down sides, then cut notches

bolt or lag screw

double line checkering tool

file down sides then cut notches

single line checkering tool

Checkering tools.

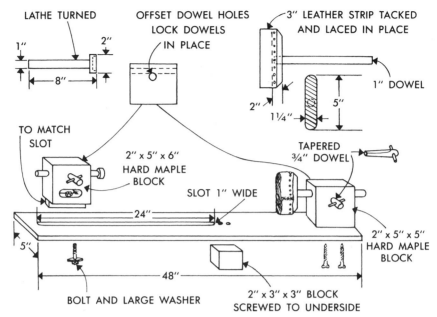

Checkering cradle.

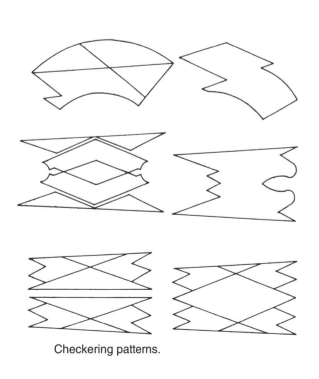

Checkering patterns.

pattern on the stock. Then use a sharp awl to scribe the pattern onto the gunstock. To get the proper shaped diamonds, the starting lines must be properly located on the pattern. Mark the end and beginning of the first line, and hold a stiff piece of plastic or heavy cardboard on the line. Use a single-line checkering tool to start the first line. Make sure the line is deep enough and straight, because all lines will follow this first starting line. The checkering tool works mostly on the "push stroke" and the strokes should be smooth and even, not choppy, the full length of the line; otherwise, the cut will be uneven and wavy.

With the first starting line made, use a "following" checkering tool to make the rest of the lines, positioning the guide side of the tool in the starting lines and allowing the cutting portion to scribe and cut the next line. Move the tool to the next line and continue.

The second starting line (diagonally across the first series of lines) is made in the same manner, using a flexible straightedge, then

First step is to use lining tools to start checkering, then use a "following tool" to create the even spaced lines.

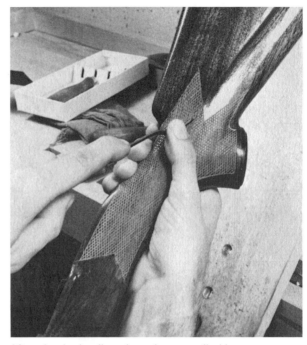

After checkering lines have been applied in one direction, change and checker in the opposite direction to create the diamond pattern.

the rest of the diamonds are cut completely. After rough cutting the diamonds, you may wish to go back and recut some areas to even up all of them. The hardest part of the checkering is keeping inside the border. This sounds simple, but when you get in a hard spot and apply a bit of pressure, it's very easy to slip past the outline. You may wish to outline the checkering pattern with a fine veining chisel or with the single edge checkering tool; but on the finer checkering works the outline is left off, the checkering itself stopping at the proper moment.

After the checkering is completed, the area of the checkering is given a light sanding with extremely fine sandpaper to cut down any burrs that might have been created. Then the checkerboard pattern of the stock is refinished with a stock finish to match the rest of the stock.

The final, finished checkering.

2

Muzzle-loaders and Accessories

One of the most satisfying pieces of outdoor equipment the sportsman can build is a black-powder muzzle-loading rifle. These historic guns are challenging to build and fun to shoot. There are many different kits available, containing all the components and an unfinished stock, or if you prefer you can custom-build one from scratch. Either way, the finished product will be something you'll not only enjoy for years in the field, but will be mighty proud to hang over your fireplace and say "I built that one."

The biggest problem in making up your own gun is acquiring the right wood for the stock. Traditionally muzzleloader stocks have been made from maple or walnut. The main thing is that the wood should be dense, close grained, and fairly straight through the barrel channel. Not only should the stock blank be sound with no cracks or open knot holes, it should also be thoroughly seasoned, preferably kiln dried. Many stock builders prefer to make their stock out of a piece of wood they've picked up in the field. In this case, make sure you allow the wood to season for at

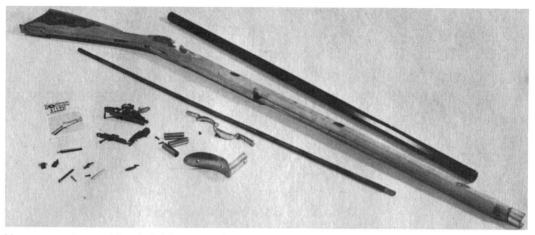

You can purchase a kit to build the gun or build it from separate components.

least three years in a cool, dry place such as the top of a garage.

After acquiring the blank, the next step is to cut it to shape. Make the pattern for the stock and use a bandsaw to rough-cut the outline. Then mark the inlet areas with a felt-tip pen and rout these out using a small electric hand-held grinder. This is the hardest and trickiest part. The objective in any gun inletting is to get the areas cut out so the parts will fit properly without any binding, yet not leave any open spaces for oil, dirt, or debris to get in. In addition, the wood and metal mating surfaces must be flush. Cut the stock somewhat oversize, then start fitting the metal pieces in place. After that it's a matter of fitting, filing, shaping, and refitting, often many, many times until you have a smooth blend of wood and metal. The task will take several hours of work, but if done properly it will reveal craftsmanship of the highest caliber.

With the stock rough-cut to shape, fit the butt plate and patch box in place. These are made of brass and the butt plate is rough shaped. It must be shaped along with the butt of the stock to fit smoothly and blend in with the patch box. Using a grinder or metal file, cut the butt plate down to match. Incidentally, you can also cut the wooden butt down

at the same time to give a smooth even blend of the two. Use a polishing wheel with buffing compound to polish both the wood and metal down to a smooth surface. This will take a bit of time, but will result in an extremely beautiful finished appearance.

When all is polished thoroughly with no scratch or file marks, remove the butt plate and the patch box and set them aside. When using a screwdriver on finished metal parts, make sure the screwdriver fits the screws. A

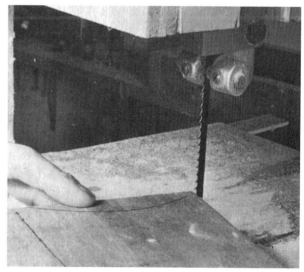

Bandsaw out the stock.

And shape it using rasps, portable grinders, etc.

Screw the butt plate and patch box in place after inletting with grinder, then grind down or file to fit the stock. The ground down butt plate and patch box are polished to a sheen using buffing compounds on a polishing wheel.

too small or too large screwdriver will only cause you to slip and gouge the finished metal surface.

Place the barrel in a vise and screw the barrel tang into the end of the barrel. Use a pair of vise-grip pliers or other hard-gripping pliers and turn the tang in as far as it will go. Make sure that the top of the tang (normally

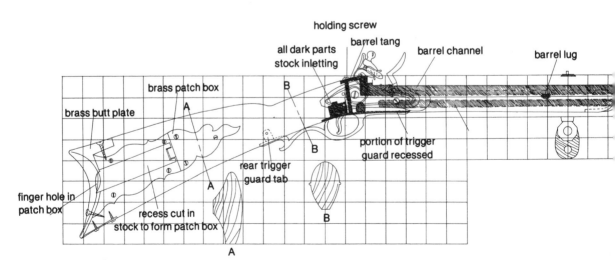

Stock pattern, 1" squares.

the flat spot) lines up with the top flat of the barrel.

Fit the barrel into the barrel channel. This may take a bit of inletting (cutting the channel to match the barrel). Use small wood chisels to cut away any parts of the barrel that need to be. Make sure that the barrel fits snugly into the barrel channel, and that there are no obstructions or raised wood to keep the barrel up off the bottom of the barrel channel. The amount of fine carving done here will be reflected in the accuracy of the gun. Wrap masking tape around the barrel and the barrel stock to hold the barrel securely in place, then bore a starting hole for the screw that holds the tang and barrel in place. Temporarily fasten the barrel in place by installing the tang screw.

The barrels will be prebored with tiny holes for the holding pins that hold the barrel in the channel. Inlet the brass escutcheon plates, bore through them and the sides of the barrel channel making sure that the holes line up with the holes in the bottom of the barrel. Drive small brass pins in place to hold the barrel in the channel temporarily.

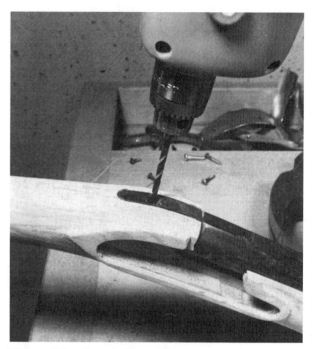

Fit barrel into barrel channel, make sure there are no obstructions and that it fits down snugly. Bore screw hole for tang screw.

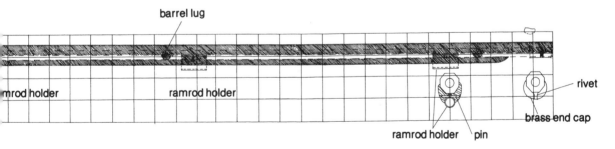

barrel lug

mrod holder   ramrod holder

ramrod holder   pin

rivet

brass end cap

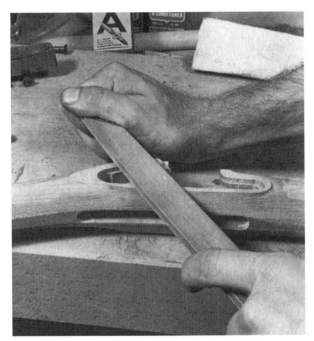

When all metal parts are temporarily fitted in place, mark wood areas, remove metal parts, and shape area around lock and other metal parts. Then shape rest of stock to suit.

File a finger notch in the side of the butt plate facing the patch box. This enables you to flip open the patch box more easily.

Screw the side escutcheons and the lock in place and mark all areas for removal of wood to blend down with the metal parts. Take off all metal pieces and remove as much wood as needed, using a rasp or small portable electric hand-grinder. Remove only a little wood at a time, replace the metal parts, and remove more as needed. When all metal parts will fit properly, remove them for the final time and sand the stock thoroughly. Use progressively finer grits of sandpaper to get a glass-smooth finish.

Wipe the wood surface with a damp cloth to raise any wood grain. If you wish to carve portions of the stock, do so at this time. Sand down any raised grain, allow the wood to dry thoroughly, then wipe with a tack cloth (a smooth cloth dipped in varnish, then squeezed almost dry). This will remove any sanding dust, dirt, or other debris.

Stain the stock. If using a maple stock, a good color combination would be equal parts of maple and walnut stain. This gives the old-fashioned look to the gun. You can use a penetrating or a nonpenetrating oil stain; either will do a good job. Although the penetrating oil will give a smoother blend, it may be a bit dark.

Apply a good gunstock finish either by hand, if using one of the older finishes, or by spraying on one of the newer plastic finishes. Apply several light coats and use extra-fine steel wool between coats to rub the stock down to a smooth, satiny sheen. After the last coat, apply paste wax and buff it to a hard sheen with steel wool, followed by a soft cloth.

After the stock is finished completely, replace the metal parts starting with the patch box. Position the trigger assembly in place and screw it securely to the stock when it fits properly. Again, this part may take an extra bit of sanding and filing to allow the

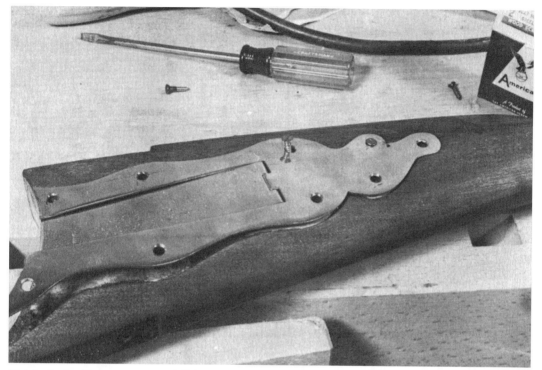

Finish stock with epoxy gunstock finish, then refasten patch box and butt plate in place.

Fit the trigger assembly in place, then install trigger guard. It should be buffed on the polishing wheel first. Note use of proper size screwdriver. Use the proper size when working on guns.

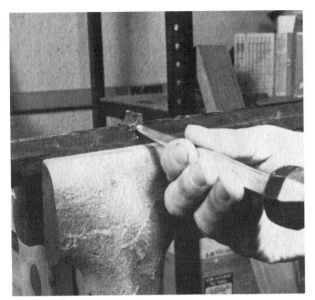

Tap rear and front sights into barrel. Using a soft punch and a hammer, drive from the left side.

Replace barrel back in barrel channel, screw in tang screw, and tap in brass pins. File pins off smooth with escutcheon plates.

assembly to clear the inside channel for the trigger to work properly. When it does, fasten the trigger guard in place. Like all brass parts of the gun, this must first be buffed on a wheel using buffing compound to bring out the sheen and give it a polished finished appearance.

Tap the rear and front sights in place. Use a soft metal punch for this job and drive in from the left side. Don't try to sight in the rifle at this time, merely get the sights in position.

Replace the metal escutcheons in the inletted holes in the stock, drive brass pins in place and peen them over slightly, then file down smooth. Fit the lock in position and screw in the holding screws. The lock is held in place with holding screws from the opposite side.

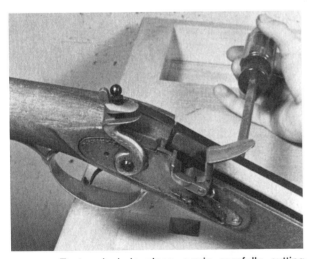

Fasten lock in place, again carefully cutting away wood that may not allow lock to fit properly. Lock is held in place by screws on opposite side.

The stock can be further decorated by inletting pieces of brass into it.

MUZZLELOADING ACCESSORIES

Part of the fun of muzzleloading comes from making and using the traditional accessories.

Ramrod

The ramrod is made from a rounded and tapered piece of oak stock. Cut it to shape and smooth with progressively finer grits of sandpaper. The ramrod should fit your particular barrel size without binding in any way, but should not be so thin that pressure can't be applied to drive home the patched ball. Ramrods are traditionally finished with a candy-striped appearance. To do this, wrap a ⅜-inch piece of rawhide around the ramrod, leaving ⅜-inch spacing between the strips, then use a torch to scorch the ramrod. Remove the rawhide, sand the ramrod smooth, and finish with several coats of paste wax.

Powder Horn

Probably the best-known accessory is the powder horn. For this you will need a steer or cow horn, readily available from slaughterhouses. One method is to get fresh horns and place them outside in a safe place where dogs and other animals can't get to them, and allow them to rot and "cure" for about six months. They can be cleaned up fairly easy in this manner. A better way is to boil the horn for about two hours, then place the horn portion in a vise and cut around the base, but not through the center section. Then you can pull the center section out. Again, the horn should dry and cure for a couple of months before you attempt to make the powder horn. After the horn has cured, the outside should be rasped down and all roughness removed. A rasp in a portable electric sander makes this job fast and easy; then use a flap sander to cut away the rasp marks. Follow with a buffing wheel and "white compound" to put the final polish on the horn. You can also do this job with steel wool but it takes a lot of time and patience to get the satiny, glass-smooth finish.

Cut off the top end of the horn and turn down a base plug on a lathe. You can use a brass ring at the top of the plug to tie a thong to, or turn the plug with a thong holder. Smooth and polish while still in the lathe. Heat the horn in boiling water and dry it thoroughly, then fit the plug in place. Use epoxy glue to fasten the plug in the horn. You can also bore small holes through the horn and drive decorative tacks through the horn into the base plug as an extra decoration as well as for providing more holding power.

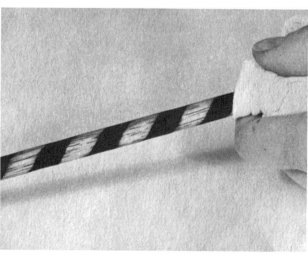

Make a ramrod from a piece of oak, tapering it and rounding it to fit down in the barrel properly. Then wrap it with rawhide and burn the stripes in with a torch. Remove rawhide, sand and polish the ramrod.

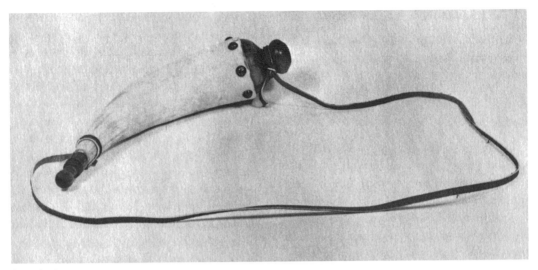

Powder horn.

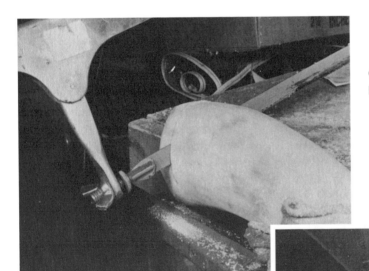

Cut base and end square, then cut pointed end square.

Turn a base plug to fit down in base and glue it in place with epoxy glue. Small holes can be bored in horn and decorative tacks driven into wooden plug.

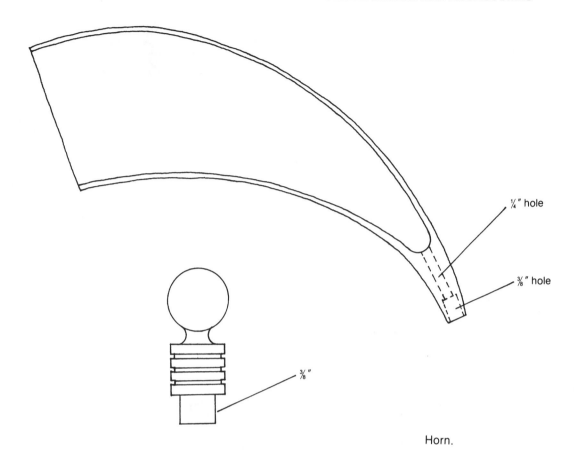

¼″ hole

⅜″ hole

⅜″

Horn.

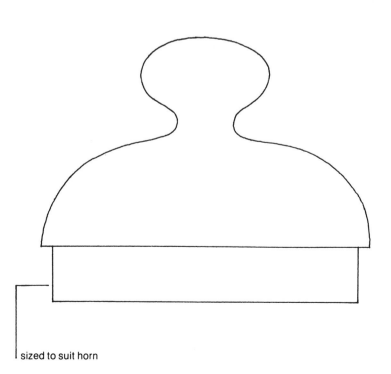

sized to suit horn

The small end of the horn can be shaped in many different ways. It can be filed into various shapes, to hold the opposite end of the carrying thong, for example, or it can be left plain. In any case, cut it off square. A small wooden peg can be turned and fitted in the end of the horn, or you can purchase a pouring spout of brass and fit it in the horn. Bore a starting hole in the end with a tiny starting drill, then follow with a larger bit as shown. Fit the plug in place, tie on the carrying strap, and you're ready. Some builders like to etch their name and the date in the horn using a hot knife blade.

With horn shaped and bored, turn down an end plug of hardwood and push it in place. Finish horn with polish.

Pouring your own "bullets" is easy. Use a purchased mold in a caliber that will fit your particular gun. Merely melt lead in a ladle and pour into the mold. Allow to cool and remove lead balls.

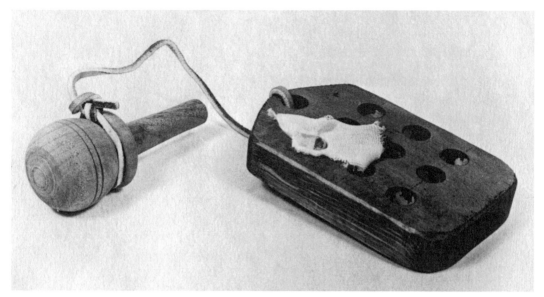

Make a ball starter and block from hardwood.

LOADING BLOCK

One of the handiest projects you can build for your muzzleloader is a loading block and ball starter. The block is nothing more than a ¾-inch-thick piece of hardwood such as oak or walnut. Bore holes in the block to hold the patched balls firmly. The holes should be small enough so the balls won't fall out, but they should not be so small that they will cause the balls to become distorted.

The ball starter can be turned on a lathe or whittled out. The tip of the ball starter should be small enough to push the patched balls out of the block and into the muzzleloader barrel. Attach the ball starter to the block with a 9-inch length of leather.

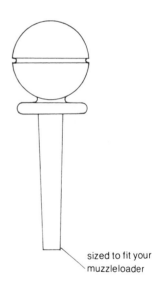

sized to fit your
muzzleloader

holes sized to fit your muzzleloader

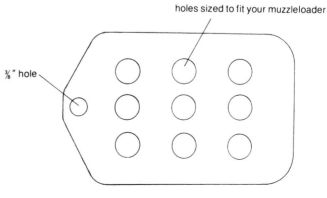

⅜" hole

3

Knives and Accessories

The art of making knives is one of man's oldest crafts, and today is enjoying a real renaissance. Beautiful and practical custom knives can be made by almost anyone with a little effort and practice, and making them doesn't require a lot of equipment. The good thing about building your own knife is that the knife can be designed for just your particular needs. To many sportsmen, the appeal of building knives is the same as tinkering with fine guns—you get both woodworking and metalworking challenges.

If designed properly and built with care and attention to details, a custom-made knife will not only serve its owner for a lifetime, but can be passed down from generation to generation as a heritage piece. My father has several skinning and caping knives handmade by a great uncle, and some of the knives are over fifty years old.

Forging the blade for a custom knife is beyond the capabilities of most home knife builders, but getting the blade is no real problem. There are several sources for ready-made knife blades as well as knifemaking materials. The devout do-it-yourselfer can easily grind

These old-time skinning, caping, and butchering knives were handmade, and a couple of them are over fifty years old.

blades from discarded metal items. These should be of a high-carbon steel, tough enough to resist breakage from dropping, yet hard enough to hold an edge. This type of steel will polish up as beautiful as any expensive blade from a sporting-goods store rack. With use, however, this steel will mottle and discolor to an even (rust-resisting) dark brown. Although not as pretty as many of the stainless steel and other exotic metal blades, they will last long and will provide a good cutting edge that can easily be resharpened without rolling over or flaking off in tiny steel splinters.

One good source for blade material is discarded metal-working files. Industrial files make the best blades because they're bigger and give a thicker, larger piece of metal to make a knife blade from. Avoid cheap files; they are too brittle and will snap and break too easily. Another source of blade metal is discarded industrial hacksaw blades. For thinner blades, for filleting or paring, or kitchen knife blades, try an old "key-hole" or "wall-saw" blade. These are usually hard enough to provide plenty of edge, yet are tough and springy.

After learning the basics of using a purchased blade, the knifemaker will want to try out designs of his own and build a custom knife that expresses his artistic sense and practical needs.

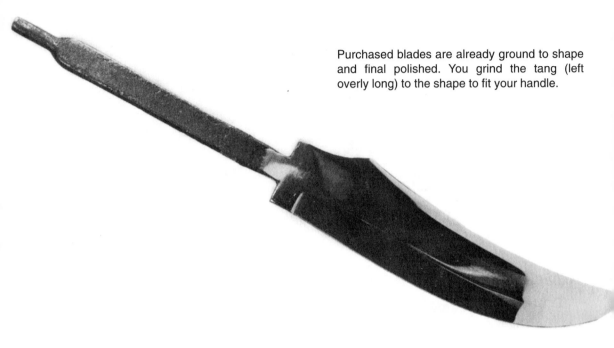

Purchased blades are already ground to shape and final polished. You grind the tang (left overly long) to the shape to fit your handle.

HUNTING KNIVES

One of the easiest and more practical hunting knives for the beginner to make has a handle of elk antler. The handle comes from the heavy butt end of the antler, close to the skull. The elk hunter, especially, will enjoy a hunting knife with a handle from a big bull he's collected. You can make the knife using a purchased blade or one ground out yourself. Details for making your own blades are given later in the chapter.

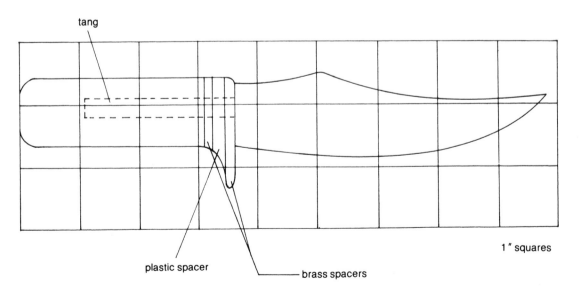

tang

plastic spacer

brass spacers

1 ″ squares

Bone handle knife.

The first step in building such a knife is to grind the tang of the purchased blade square, so it will fit properly in a hole drilled in the bone handle. The tang on most purchased knives is usually long and must be ground off to the length you wish for your handle. With the tang shaped as you desire, cut and drill a piece of brass to make a finger guard. If you wish to add some frills, drill two pieces of brass to fit down over the tang, with a piece of plastic sandwiched between them. When drilling through the brass spacers, make sure you've got them clamped tightly. Soft metal such as brass can catch easily when the drill bit goes through and will end up whirling around on the end of the drill bit at dangerous speeds. Try the finger-guard spacers to make sure they will fit down over the tang.

Drill the bone handle to enable the tang to fit down in it snugly and firmly. The tang shouldn't fit too tight, or you may crack the

Clamp the blade in a vise. Smear epoxy between brass spacers, fill hole in bone handle with epoxy. Place spacers down on tang, force bone handle down onto tang.

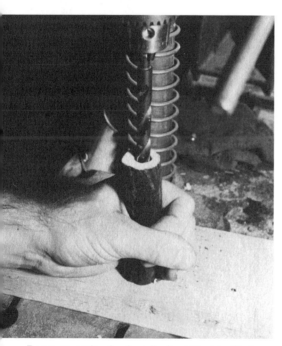

Bone or antler for handle is drilled to fit down over tang. Use the slowest speed on drill press and make a small starting hole, gradually enlarging to fit tang. Holding in a wood clamp is safer than holding by hand.

bone. Make sure that you don't drill completely through the bone, but just deep enough to enable the tang to slip in completely.

You can drill this hole by clamping the bone in a vise and using a variable-speed electric drill, but the easiest method and the one ensuring a good, straight hole in the handle is to use a drill press—clamping the bone in a wood clamp—or holding it securely. It must be held firmly in position so that the tang hole will be drilled straight and true in the handle. The pithy center of the antler is actually quite easy to drill.

Clamp the blade in a vise, making sure that the tang points straight up and is plumb in all directions. Position the first brass finger-guard spacer in place. Mix a small amount of a two-part epoxy glue and smear it on the

The cured "knife" handle may then be filed to shape, smoothed with progressively finer sandpaper, and finally buffed on a buffing wheel held in an electric drill clamped in a vise.

Work the tang in the hole to ensure that all areas are covered thoroughly, then wipe off excess glue. Make sure that the handle is pushed down on the spacers and the spacers pushed tightly together, then allow the glue to set for at least twenty-four hours.

The cured handle may then be shaped using files, rasps, or a small grindstone. When the handle shape suits your grip, smooth it and the finger guard down using progressively finer grits of sandpaper. A final polish can be applied with the use of a buffing wheel, but be sure to hold the knife firmly and keep it low on the buffing wheel. Always keep the edge of the blade turned down and away from the wheel, or it may catch and be jerked from your hands.

A variation of this knife utilizes the brass finger guard, plus a brass cap on the end. The center handle section can be either bone or wood, or even rings of leather glued together on the metal tang. In making this type of knife, the tang is left long enough to reach into the brass cap. The end of the tang is ground to form a round end. This is then threaded, a hole drilled in the brass cap, and the hole threaded to match the threads on the tang. To assemble the knife, smear glue over all portions and place them in position, then turn the brass cap down over the threaded

brass spacer. Smear both sides of the plastic spacer and both sides of the next brass spacer, then slip into position. Work the epoxy glue into the hole in the handle and smear it on the tang, then slowly push the tang into the hole, allowing the excess glue to squeeze out.

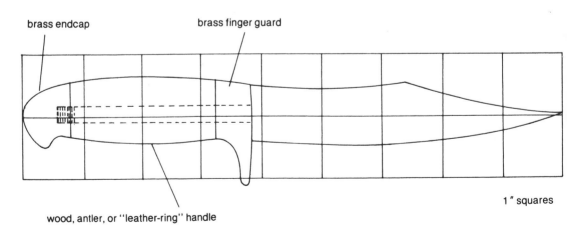

brass endcap

brass finger guard

wood, antler, or "leather-ring" handle

1″ squares

Another style of knife uses brass spacers for the finger guard, amaranth wood for the handle, and a brass cap on the top. This small "paring knife" makes a small, practical, and beautiful hunting knife.

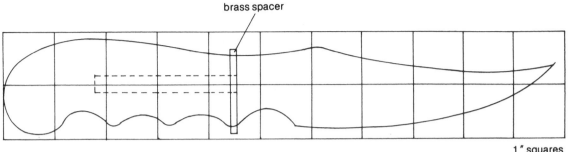

brass spacer

1 ″ squares

tang. It's a good idea to assemble and glue the knife unfinished, allow it to dry, then rasp and shape it, blending metal to wood or bone to make a nice smooth transition.

Another style of knife utilizes a wooden handle and is made in much the same manner as the first bone-only handle. It is simple, easy to build, and will produce a beautiful and practical knife. A hard, dense oily wood such as rosewood, amaranth, or zebrawood should be used. Again, the handle is glued

You can also easily make the entire knife. Use an old industrial file for the blade, grinding it to any shape or style you desire.

Another style of knife uses a wood handle without brass finger guard and cap.

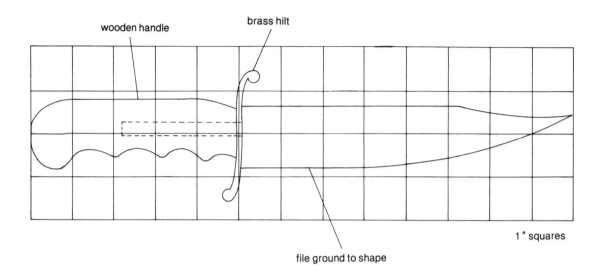

wooden handle

brass hilt

1 ″ squares

file ground to shape

down over the tang. A rounded finger guard may be placed between the wooden handle and the blade.

The blade on the knife shown has a built-in "front fingerhole"; thus the handle has places for only three fingers.

BLADES

Once you're able to build different handles on knives, the next step is to start building your own blades as well. An old industrial file makes the best blade, and is easily shaped if you have a small tool grinder or grindstone. The metal in a file is extremely hard, so have a pan of water handy and keep dipping the file in the water to keep it cool as you grind. The knife shown has a fat wedge shape and is extremely heavy, but it makes a great substitute for an axe when backpacking. I also carry a tiny razor-sharp hunting knife or folding knife for skinning and other camp chores.

The angle or shape of the edge of the knife depends on what it is to be used for. A hunting knife edge can run anywhere from 25 to 45 degrees of angle on the edge, depending on its purpose.

To produce a razor-sharp edge on any knife, it should be honed on a good stone of fine grit. The stone should be securely fas-

tened to a benchtop, so you can work the knife blade against it with pressure. Stroke the blade down and toward the edge using enough pressure to push material off the hone. Use both hands, one on the back of the blade and one on the handle. Many people

After the blade has been ground to shape, an edge can be put on it using a single-cut mill-bastard file.

don't apply enough pressure when honing. Stroke a few times on one side, then turn the blade over and stroke the opposite side. Try to do the same number of strokes on each side to keep the blade edge even. The hone should be kept well lubricated with light oil or water. I like to use a penetrating oil such as WD-40, which is extremely light and does a great lubricating job, yet doesn't gum up the stone.

SKINNING OR CAPING KNIVES

Another style of knife has a full-handle blade rather than a blade with a tang; the blade runs the full width of the handle and the handle pieces are fastened to each side of the blade, usually by rivets. The entire handle and blade is then shaped as desired. This style of knife is not to be confused with the thin, cheap imitation kitchen knives now on the market. The old-time knives were the knives that helped our forefathers tame a wild land and provide food for their tables.

You can also make this knife from either purchased blades (in a number of patterns) or from scratch, building the blade from a heavy-gauge, discarded saw blade or thin industrial file.

Blades for skinning and caping knives are available from a number of sources, or you can make your own from heavy-gauge, discarded saw blades, or thin industrial files.

Because of the exposure to constant moisture, a dense, oily hardwood such as amaranth, rosewood, zebrawood, or hickory should be used to make the handle. To prevent moisture from being trapped, no glue is applied between the blade and the handle. The handle is applied using hollow brass rivets. (These rivets may be purchased as

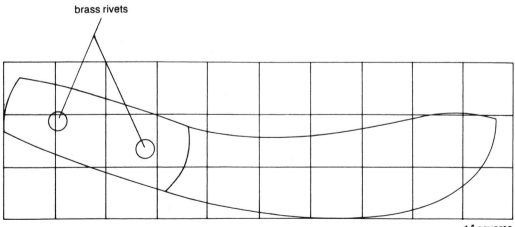

brass rivets

1 ″ squares

Handles for "butcher" or skinning knives are cut from resawn blocks of rosewood, walnut, or oak.

Blades and handles are clamped together and drilled for brass rivets.

well.) Cut the handle blanks to about 5/16 inch thick and a little bit wider than the blade. Drill the holes for the rivets, clamping a handle blank to the blade and using the holes in the blade as a pattern. (If you're making the blade yourself, omit this step, but clamp the two sides and the blade together and drill all three at once.) Drill the other handle side.

To set the rivets flush with the handle surface, they must be recessed in the handle. One of the easiest ways of doing this is to use a No. 8 countersink. Counterbore with this in a drill press on the rough side of the blanks. These holes should be drilled just deep enough to allow the rivet heads to set flush.

A homemade riveting set helps to hold all the rivet pieces and get them hammered together without denting or damaging the surrounding wood. The riveting tool is actually two lengths of steel rod that are the same diameter as the rivets. One length of rod is set in a steel block and acts as a sort of anvil. The other steel rod is a small punch. By using this tool, you're able to drive the hollow rivets together without damaging the surrounding wood.

After the handle blanks have been riveted to the blade, rasp and file the handle to the shape desired, rounding all edges to provide a uniform grip. Fine wet or dry sandpaper and a bit of linseed oil will provide a smooth fin-

A homemade punch and anvil helps in assembling riveted knives.

Rivet tops and bottoms are easily placed in position and hammered together using the homemade punch and anvil.

One fun and easy knife project is a fillet knife.

ish. Give them a final going over with linseed oil and extremely fine steel wool.

FILLET KNIVES

The blade of a fillet knife should be made from some tough, springy metal. The blade should sharpen easily, yet hold a good edge when used against bone and tough fish scales. One of the best materials for making a fillet knife blade is a discarded key-hole or wall-saw blade. These are usually made of high-carbon steel and make up a fillet knife blade that is flexible enough to bend and slide along a backbone. Yet the metal can easily be sharpened to a razor-sharp edge. The key-hole saw blade is the appropriate size, and can be ground to the shape of a fillet knife blade without a lot of grinding.

One problem with most factory-made fillet knives is that the handle is too small and doesn't provide enough grip when it becomes wet. A good fillet knife handle should fill the palm of your hand providing something solid to grasp. It should be a flat shape to prevent the blade from turning when making sideways slicing cuts. If the fillet knife is to be used as a boat knife, a leather thong for slipping over your wrist to prevent losing it is an important accessory.

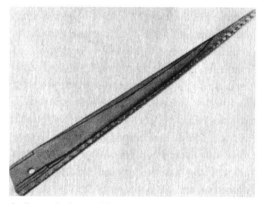

A discarded saw blade from a key-hole saw or wall saw makes the best blades for fillet knives.

top view

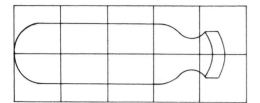

blade

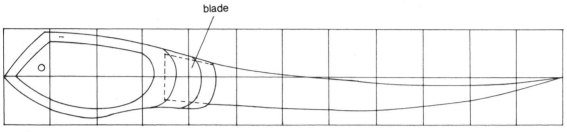

Fillet knife

1 ″ squares

Enlarge the pattern shown onto a piece of thin cardboard and cut the knife blade and handle patterns to shape. Place the cardboard blade pattern on the discarded saw blade and trace around the pattern using a crayon or grease pencil.

The blade may be ground or filed to shape. If using a file, clamp the blade tightly in a vise and use only a brand-new, single-cut file. Of course, the easiest way is to grind the blade to shape on a shop grinder or grindstone. Keep a pan of water nearby and continue dipping the blade in the water to keep it cool. If the blade becomes hot enough to discolor at any point, it will be ruined.

Grind or file the blade to the marked outline, but do not taper the edge or sharpen the blade. The butt end of the blade extends up into the handle a couple of inches, and should be left as is or roughly ground to the shape of the front of the handle.

When you have shaped the blade to suit, lay it aside and start on the handle. A fillet knife handle should be a hard, oily, and moisture-resistant wood such as amaranth,

rosewood, or zebrawood. The first step is to cut a rectangular block the size of the handle. Mark the center of the front of the handle for the saw cut. Make the slot that the blade fits in using either a band saw or a fine backsaw. The butt of the blade should fit into the slot fairly tightly. With the front slot cut, enlarge the squared drawing for the handle and transfer it to the square handle block. Using a band saw or coping saw, cut out the handle.

Smear a two-part epoxy cement over the butt of the blade and force the blade into the slot, moving it back and forth to ensure that all parts of the blade and handle slot are covered with cement. Allow the glued blade to set for at least twelve hours.

Using rasps and files, shape the handle, rounding all edges to make a smooth, comfortable grip. When the handle fits your hand comfortably, smooth it by using progressively finer grits of sandpaper.

With the blade and handle assembled and the handle shaped, the next step is to grind or file down the edge of the blade. The cutting

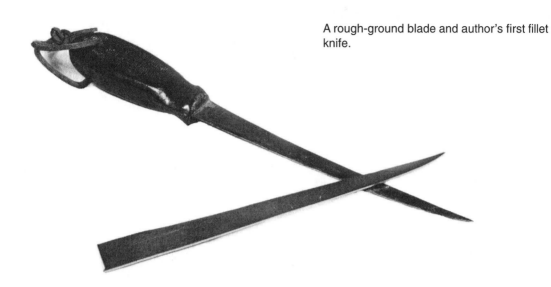

A rough-ground blade and author's first fillet knife.

The fillet knife handle should be cut from a block of hard, oily wood such as amaranth, zebra-wood, or rosewood.

The blade fits in a slot cut in the front of the handle, and this should be cut first, then the handle blank sawn out.

Fasten the blade and handle together with epoxy cement.

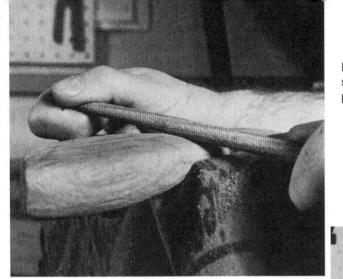

File the handle to the shape desired, then smooth with progressively finer grits of sandpaper.

Thin down the edge of the blade, tapering it to about 5 or 10 degrees. Do this equally on both sides of the blade to produce a good sharp edge.

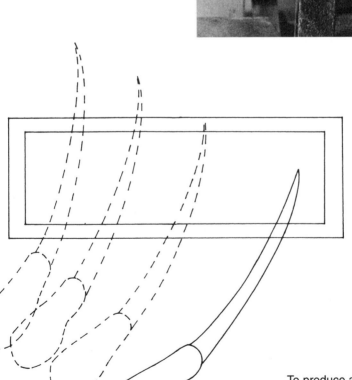

To produce a razor-sharp edge on the fillet knife, it should be honed on a good stone. The drawing shows the proper stroking on the stone.

edge of the blade should be thinned down to about a 5- to 10-degree angle or taper. When both sides of the blade have been tapered and thinned down so that they meet to produce a sharp edge, hone the blade on a good stone. Use a penetrating oil as a lubricant on the stone and fasten the stone to a solid workbench or tabletop.

If the knife is to be used as a boat knife, you may wish to checker it with checkering tools to provide a more nonslip grip. You can also drill a hole in the upper end and tie a loop of rawhide through it for slipping over your wrist.

If the handle is made from an oily wood, you may decide not to finish it. I prefer to put a gunstock finish on the handle, since it provides more protection and keeps the wood looking better longer. Tru-Oil Gunstock Finish is one of the best and is available both as a rub-on and a spray-on finish. If you use the spray-on finish (my preference), you will have to tape the blade with masking tape to prevent spraying it.

BACKPACKERS' SURVIVAL KNIVES

If backpacking is your thing, you can make an extremely lightweight custom knife that can be strapped to your backpack, and it will be a better knife than any you can buy. Make the blade portion from a discarded key-hole saw blade, grinding or filing it to the shape you desire, then wrap the handle end with several turns of black plastic electricians' tape. Lightweight, yet effective, you'll have a knife that is ideal for peeling spuds or squirrels.

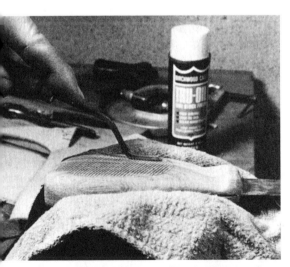

If you plan to use your fillet knife as a "boat knife," you may wish to checker the handle for a better grip. The last step is to apply a good waterproof finish.

A terrific lightweight backpacking knife can be made from a piece of heavy saw blade ground to the shape shown, taping the edge with plastic tape to provide a lightweight handle.

Some designs may require slits in back of knife sheath for belt loops.

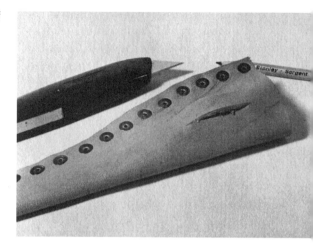

SHEATHS

Making sheaths for your custom knives is as fun and easy as making the knives. Sheaths can be made in hundreds of different patterns, sizes, and materials, but there are actually just two basic styles. One style is the familiar hanging sheath that has a loop or extension to extend the sheath below the belt. The knife is held in place by either a leather thong looped through slits and tied around its top, or by a leather strap looped through and snapped around the knife.

The second style of sheath is the pouch sheath that is patterned after the plains Indians' style of knife sheath. This type of sheath extends up past the finger guard or hilt of the knife, almost covering the entire knife. Just a small portion of the knife handle is allowed to project above the end of the sheath. The pouch sheath allows for quick and fast usage of the knife, yet keeps it from falling out or snagging on brush, without being tied or snapped in place. Pouch sheaths were usually made of lighter-weight leather than hanging sheaths, and those on a brave's loincloth loop were decked out in fancy beadwork or quill work.

The sheath patterns shown are to fit the particular knife patterns shown. You can make up your own patterns using brown wrapping paper. Simply lay the knife on the paper and mark a straight line beginning at the top of the finger guard or hilt and continuing down to the tip of the knife. Extend past the knife tip at least ¾ inch. Now mark the shape of the knife leaving at least ½-inch clearance around the blade. If you're making a pouch sheath, leave more clearance especially around the handle to provide for its thickness. The resulting pattern is one half of your knife sheath. Mark this on a sheet of paper, then fold it over and mark the other side.

The leather for knife sheaths should be fairly stiff, a mediumweight hide, and should be about ¹⁄₁₆-inch thick. Cowhide or thick calfskin makes the best sheaths. Belly scraps left over from full hides found in leather shops make good pieces for knife and axe sheaths.

You'll need a sharp knife, preferably a shop knife with a disposable razor blade. You will also need a leather punch. If you plan to use stitching or lacing to fasten the sheath together, a regular punch will ensure correct spacing of the holes, but a sharpened nail can be used instead. If you plan to fasten the sheath with rivets, you'll need the correct size punch or one of the "star" punches that has a

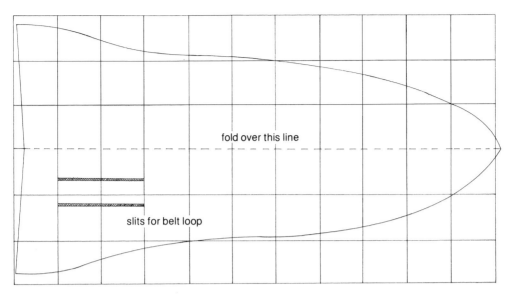

fold over this line

slits for belt loop

Fillet knife sheath

1 ″ squares

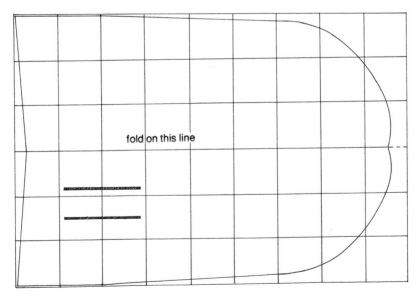

fold on this line

Caping knife sheath

1 ″ squares

Patterns for all sheaths.

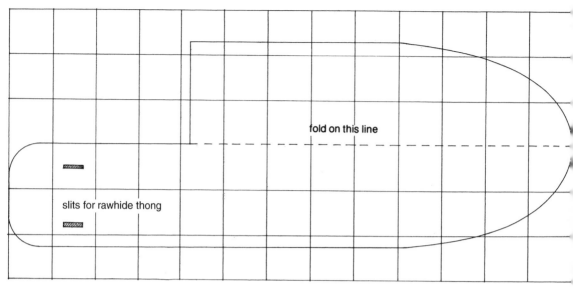

fold on this line

slits for rawhide thong

File blade knife sheath

1″ squares

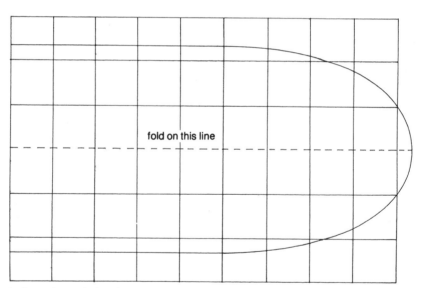

fold on this line

Indian-style pouch sheath

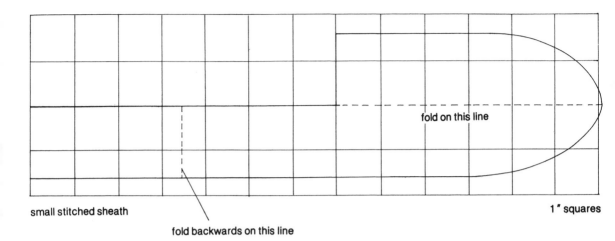

small stitched sheath

fold on this line

fold backwards on this line

1″ squares

number of different size punches on a rotating wheel. This type punch is squeezed through the leather to produce the desired hole. You will also need lacing and stitching thread needles or an automatic shoemakers' awl. The latter has the thread in a bobbin held in the handle and is used to make the popular running stitch.

There are three basic ways of fastening a leather knife sheath together. The first is lacing, which is the easiest, but also the shortest lasting. By using lacing of a contrasting color from the leather, the sheath can be made quite attractive. In lacing a sheath together, holes are punched ¼-inch apart and about ⅛-inch from the edge, holding both sides of the sheath together and punching them at the same time. When all corresponding holes are punched, the lacing is threaded through from the inside of the sheath, taken around back and brought through to the front. The lacing is then taken in and out around the edge. Make sure you have enough lacing for the job. Each loop should be pulled tightly in place as it is laced, but not tight enough to pucker or cause distortion of the leather. When the edge of the sheath is reached, the lacing is tied off and the end clipped and slipped into the sheath. If the sheath is designed with an end

loop for a belt, you'll want to lace this as well, to continue the design of the lacing.

The second but somewhat more formal looking way of fastening a sheath together is to stitch it. This type of fastening lasts longer than lacing, but stitching can rot or be cut by a sharp blade.

There are any number of stitches that can be used, but the most popular is the running

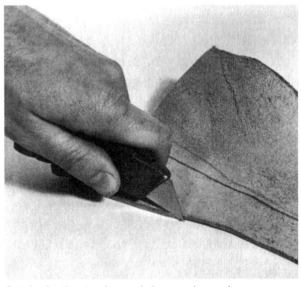

Cut the leather to size and shape using a sharp razor blade in a holder.

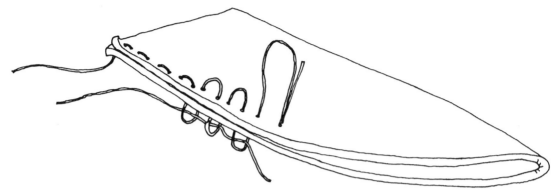

This type of sheath can be stitched using a leatherworker's awl and a running stitch as shown.

stitch. Two needles are used for this stitch, one needle to run the thread through the punched holes while another is used on the underside of the sheath to run a length of thread through the loops made by the first needle. Both threads are then drawn taut making a tight, attractive stitch. An automatic awl will do this type of stitch quickly and easily. The only thing to remember in stitching is to make sure the end threads are securely tied off so they can't slip and allow the stitching to unravel.

The third method—unattractive to many, but decorative in its own way—is fastening with rivets. This is a particularly good way of fastening a sheath to be used for a fillet or boat knife, because the constant moisture will rot the threads in a stitched sheath. Riveted sheaths have the longest life. To make riveted sheaths more attractive, you can place the rivets extremely close together, giving them a decorative rather than a functional look.

In assembling a riveted sheath, the first step is to punch the holes for the rivets. This should be done with the appropriate size rivet punch, punching the holes for the two sides of the sheath at the same time. Place the bottom portion of the rivet on a solid surface, push the two leather edges together, place the top rivet in place, and tap with a hammer to close the rivet. It's as simple as that. Continue until the sheath is finished.

If the sheath is to be riveted, use a punch of the appropriate size and punch the holes.

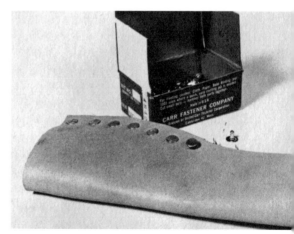

Punch each hole, fit rivet, then punch succeeding holes.

Rivets are closed using a hammer and solid backing such as an anvil or metal plate.

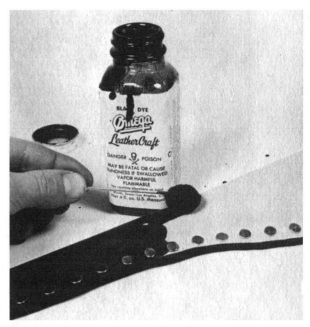

To make the sheath more attractive, you can dye it almost any color of the rainbow. A coat of leather "finish" will help protect the sheath.

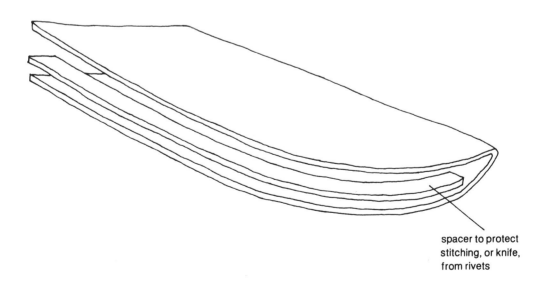

spacer to protect stitching, or knife, from rivets

You can also make an excellent axe sheath from scraps left over from making sheaths for your knives.

If the knife has an extremely sharp blade or sharp point, you can place a spacer along the edge of the sheath as shown to prevent it from cutting the stitching or lacing and to keep it from becoming dulled on the metal rivets.

A plain sheath can be made more attractive by dying it with a leather dye. Use a way-out color such as black, blue, or red, or give it a more functional color such as walnut or oak brown, blending and wiping to give the sheath an antiqued leather look. The leather should be given a coat of leather finish to protect it, then a soft wax or polishing with shoe polish.

4

Archery Tackle

THE BOW

As a kid I was always making some kind of hunting or fishing equipment and was fascinated by the bows and arrows made by the Indians. I learned that the bows made by the Osage Indians in my area were made from the wood of the Osage orange or hedge tree. Since my family's farm was bounded on three sides with the hedge, I naturally had a plentiful supply; and over the course of several years I built at least a dozen Indian-style bows. Each one was just a little bit better than the one before it. Although I used Osage orange for my bows, hickory or ash would be just as good. The Indian method was to use unseasoned wood, but I preferred seasoned wood.

If you wish to make an Indian-style bow, you will need a blank of wood 4 feet long, ½-inch thick, and about 2 inches wide. You can also purchase bow blanks of this nature, made of lemonwood, such as were used by Robin Hood and other English archers. But making your own Indian-style bows and arrows gives you a feeling of identity with the

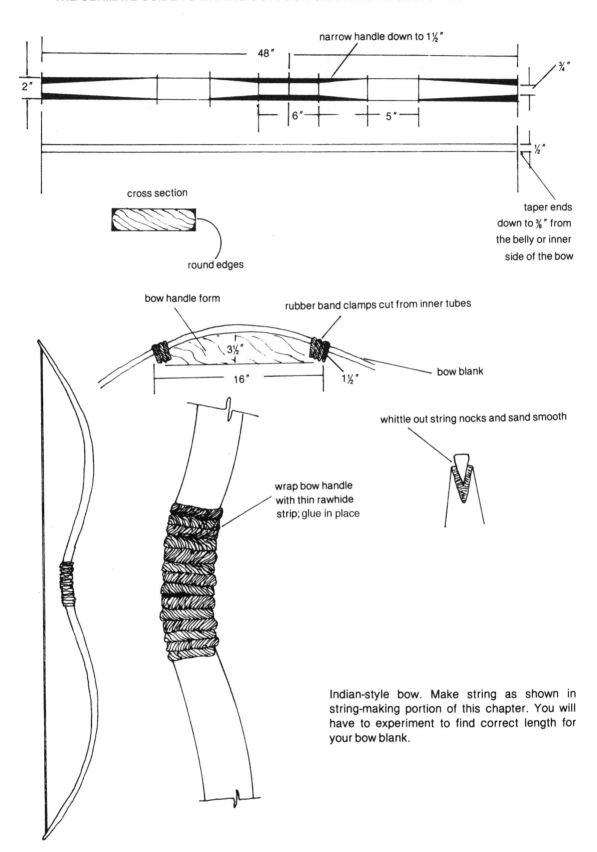

narrow handle down to 1½"

48"

2"

¾"

6"

5"

½"

cross section

round edges

taper ends down to ⅜" from the belly or inner side of the bow

bow handle form

rubber band clamps cut from inner tubes

3½"

16"

1½"

bow blank

whittle out string nocks and sand smooth

wrap bow handle with thin rawhide strip; glue in place

Indian-style bow. Make string as shown in string-making portion of this chapter. You will have to experiment to find correct length for your bow blank.

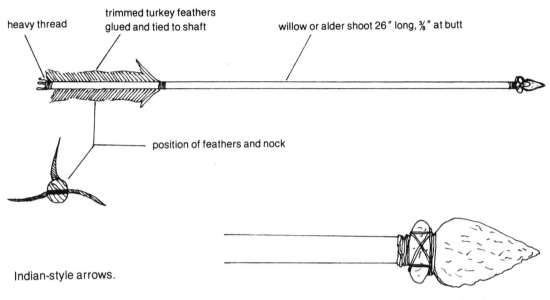

heavy thread

trimmed turkey feathers
glued and tied to shaft

willow or alder shoot 26″ long, ⅜″ at butt

position of feathers and nock

Indian-style arrows.

method of securing flint arrowhead

native Americans, and is something every true hunter and outdoorsman should experience at least once.

Enlarge the drawing of the bow onto a piece of brown paper and transfer to the bow blank. From then on it's merely a matter of whittling, rasping, and smoothing to shape the bow as shown. Once you have the bow's basic shape, make up the handle form as shown. Place the bow in hot water and allow it to soak for about an hour, changing the water as necessary to keep it hot. Then place over the handle form, tie in place, and leave overnight. The next day remove, final sand the bow, and apply a good grade of furniture polish to it, buffing with fine steel wool.

You can also make your own Indian-style arrows, although I would recommend hunting only small game with them.

Since the old-time bow and arrows won't do for big game, nor are they nearly as accurate as today's equipment, you may want to build a modern fiberglass and wood-laminated recurve bow. Although you can purchase separately all the materials needed for building such a bow, your best bet is to use one of the many bow kits on the market. These are designed to specific pull weights and sizes, and take much of the guesswork out of building the bow. Building a homemade recurve bow isn't especially hard, but it does require attention to detail and slow, patient work.

The bow shown is an all-purpose field target and hunting bow 66 inches long. It can be built in varying pull weights. The kit comes with all the necessary materials to make up the bow; however, you can use the same pattern and information shown and purchase the materials as you need to build your own bow.

You must first build a form to hold the bow solidly in position while the fiberglass and wood laminations are being glued in place. Enlarge the squared drawing for the bow glueing form, and cut the form from a piece of 1¾-inch-thick stock, preferably maple or oak. You can glue together two pieces to make the thick stock if necessary.

When cutting out, stay just on the outside of the line.

Your finished bow will only be as good as the bow form. The sawed surface of the form must be absolutely straight and square with the sides of the form and as smooth as possible. Check for accuracy with a small square and sand and file to shape. Other clamping and holding pieces include the pressure blocks and riser form, which should be cut from the scraps left from the bow form. Cut the pressure blocks 1½ × 4 inches, the riser form 1½ × 1¾ × 36 inches. Excellent clamps for assembling the bow can be cut from an old inner tube, cutting it much the same way as peeling an apple, to produce continuous 2-inch strips.

Begin the actual assembly of the bow with the handle-riser section. Cover the upper surface of the riser form with waxed paper to shed glue, and clamp it in a vise. Mark center lines around all components of the riser and position them on the form. Make a practice run with the rubber clamps. Wrap them as tightly as possible around the laminations, tucking the ends under the loops to tie off. Check that components are correctly positioned.

Homemade laminated recurve bow is not only as "good" as factory made, but provides a lot of satisfying hours in the building as well.

To glue up bow, you must have a "mold" or form. Make it up from 1¾-inch stock, preferably maple or oak.

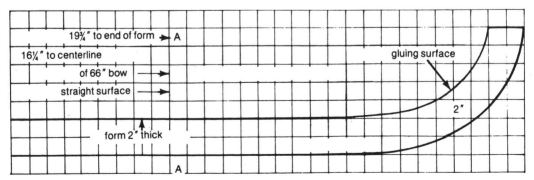

19¾" to end of form → A

16¼" to centerline

of 66″ bow →

straight surface →

form 2″ thick

gluing surface

2″

A

1″ squares

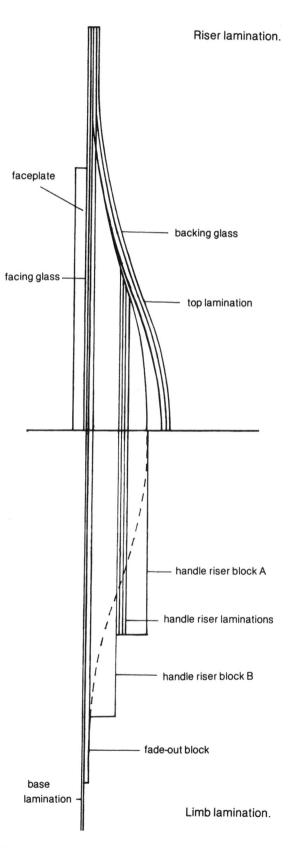

Riser lamination.

faceplate

backing glass

facing glass

top lamination

handle riser block A

handle riser laminations

handle riser block B

fade-out block

base lamination

Limb lamination.

Before applying glue, build the heat box shown. Mix the glue according to instructions and just enough for each job. (The glue used for bowmaking is URAC-185, a two-component synthetic resin.) Brush an even coat on meeting surfaces. Position the base laminations so they meet at the center of the form and stack the rest of the components in place. C-clamp the assembly so all centerline marks align. Position the base laminations parallel; strips out of line will twist the bow. Place one of the pressure blocks on the end of the fade-out block and wrap it tightly with rubber bands. Position a pressure block at the other end of the fade-out block, check the laminations for parallel, and start wrapping

Spread glue on all pieces of the handle riser assembly, place it on the riser gluing form and wrap securely with rubber-band clamps. Place in the heat box for 7 to 8 hours or until it cures.

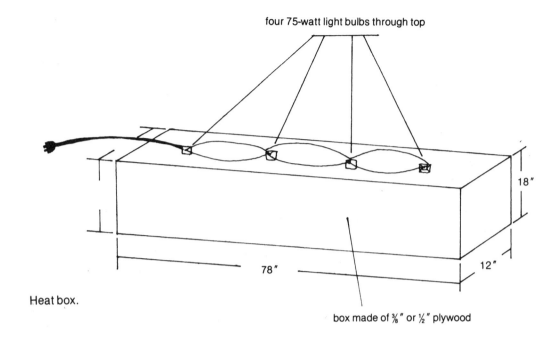

four 75-watt light bulbs through top

18"

12"

78"

Heat box.

box made of ⅜" or ½" plywood

with rubber bands. Cover the assembly with several layers of bands as shown. Place the assembly in the heat box for eight hours. Check the temperature frequently and remove a bulb or two if heat goes over 125°.

Remove the glued riser section from the form and cut the dried glue from both sides. Be careful; the dried glue cuts like a razor blade. Smooth and square up one side of the riser to the base lamination. This surface slides on the saw table, with the riser pattern on the upper surface. bandsaw the handle riser to shape. File smooth the sawed outline, keeping adjacent surfaces at right angles. Blend the ends of the fade-out blocks into the base laminations as shown.

Now that you have the handle riser laminated, do a bit of preparation before laminating the limbs. The limbs on the bow shown are laminated one at a time, using the same bow form. This gives a better balanced bow than making the complete bow in one piece. Cut two pressure pads from ⅛-inch hardboard 32 inches long. One is ½-inch wide, the other 1½ inches wide. Mark a line on both sides of the nock-reinforcement blocks ⅝ inch from the square end. They align with string-groove marks on the bow-form pattern.

Begin laying up the limb lamination. Use a knife point to start, and peel the protective strip from the coarse side of both a backing and facing fiberglass strip for one limb. Place

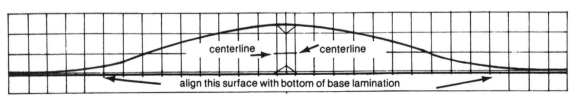

centerline   centerline

align this surface with bottom of base lamination

Riser pattern.

With a rasp and file, smooth up the band-sawed outline, blending the fade-out blocks into the base laminations.

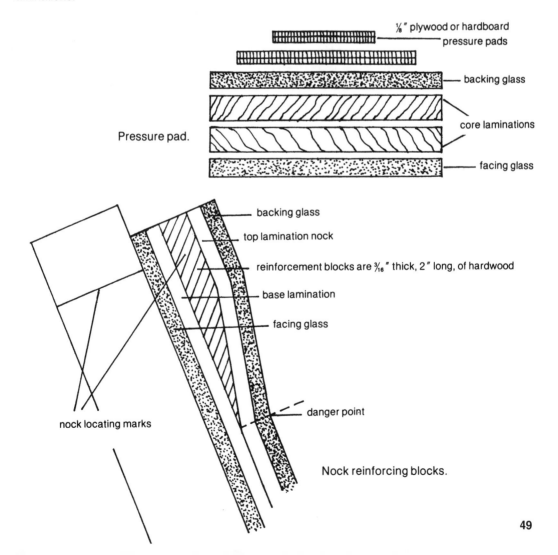

⅛" plywood or hardboard

pressure pads

backing glass

core laminations

Pressure pad.

facing glass

backing glass

top lamination nock

reinforcement blocks are ³⁄₁₆" thick, 2" long, of hardwood

base lamination

facing glass

danger point

nock locating marks

Nock reinforcing blocks.

Materials needed for bow:
2 pair of fiberglass backing strips 1¾ inches wide by sufficient thickness for bow weight
2 pair of maple core strips 1¾ inches wide by sufficient thickness for bow weight
2⅛ × 2 × 2-inch tapered tip inserts of hardwood
1 handle riser fade-out block of .300 × 1¾ × 30-inch hardwood
1 handle riser block of .700 × 1¾ × 20-inch hardwood
1 overdraw faceplate block of ½ × 1¾ × 18-inch hardwood
1 handle riser block of 1.000 × 1¾ × 15-inch hardwood
5 handle riser laminations of .050 × 1¾ × 15-inch hardwood
8 ounces of URAC-185 cement

the facing strip (coarse side up) on the bow form, then the laminated handle-riser section including the lower-core lamination, the backing glass, and the pressure pads. After a dry run, coat the pieces with glue and glue up the limb. A C-clamp at the centerline holds the pieces while you start the rubber bands. Keep the pieces aligned as you wrap. Spread the laminations at the end and push in the nock-tip reinforcing blocks, aligning marks on blocks and bow form. Wrap the assembly with rubber clamps and cure it in the heat box for eight hours, then remove from the box and season overnight. Take off the rubber bands and cut away the excess dried glued.

Glue the other limb in the same manner, butting the pieces at the centerline with the limbs parallel.

Mark an "X" on the side of the bow where the limbs align best and cover the bow-backing glass with masking tape. Cut off the ends of the bow blank at the top of each nock-reinforcement block. Clamp the blank in a vise,

masking tape up, and mark the centerline (across the bow handle) on the tape. Make a heavy mark at the midpoint of the centerline. Fasten weights to the ends of a heavy cord and stretch this over the bow so it rests on the tips of the recurves. Mark the center of one end of the bow and fit the cord over it. Lift the cord off the opposite end and move it right or left until it aligns over the mark at the center of the riser. The cord determines the axis of the length of the bow.

If the bow is straight, the cord will rest on the midpoints of each end and pass over the centerline at the midpoint of the handle. Most bows will be slightly twisted and require adjustment of the string. Do not move the string closer than 5/8-inch to either edge; try to keep the bow tips as wide as possible, yet line up the cord. After the cord is located, square a line across the bow 15 inches from the centerline. Sight along the cord so it seems to cover the heavy mark on the centerline of the riser. Mark the masking tape at the 15-inch point,

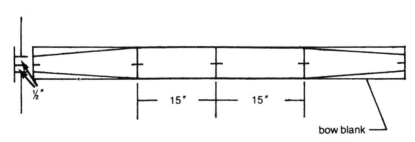

Limb guide layout.

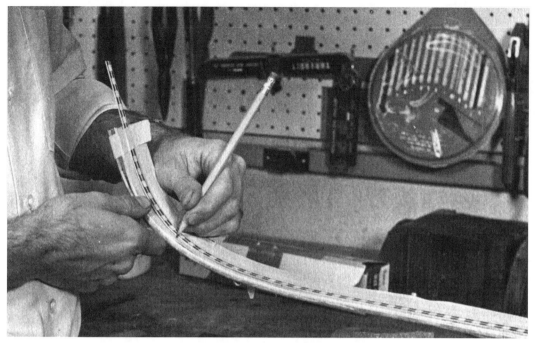

With layout marks positioned on the bow, a flexible straightedge, in this case a piece of thin wood, is used to connect the lines to get the rough shape of the bow.

where the cord appears to cover it, and repeat at the opposite end of the bow. There should now be five marks indicating the centerline (lengthwise) of the bow. If the marks at 15 inches are not on center, measure to the closest edge and mark this distance on the other

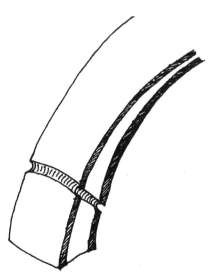

The ends of each of the limbs are marked 33 inches from the center and shallow string grooves are filed in them with a small rat-tail file.

side of the mark. Using a flexible straightedge, draw a line connecting these marks. This is the rough shape of the bow. Bandsaw the limbs to shape, using an old bandsaw blade, then remove the tape from the limbs, but not the riser. Round the edges of the glass with a fine file to keep slivers of glass from breaking off the edges as the bow is flexed.

Mark the limbs 33 inches from the centerline for the string nocks, and cut shallow grooves with a 4-inch rat-tail file. Make a work string of about sixteen to twenty strands of Dacron bowstring material. Make the work string 3 inches shorter than the bow and with large, 2-inch loops. The work and finished bowstrings are easily made on the jig shown. The Dacron strands are looped around the pegs and the two ends tied together. According to the size loops required, mark the ends as shown. Grasp the strands and pull around the pegs until the marked areas are exactly opposite the center spreader peg. Place the outside strands over the spreader peg and wrap the strands nearest you with bowstring-serving material. Wrap between the marks, tying off the thread by pulling it back through the last few loops with a loop of monofilament fishing line. Continue until both loops and arrow-contact areas are wrapped.

Mark the facing of the bow 9 inches from the center of each limb, then string the bow. Be careful, as it is quite rigid at this stage. Measure from the string to the 9-inch marks (about 5 inches); the greater distance indicates the upper limb. Mark the bow for the faceplate and rough up the area with sandpaper. Glue the assembly, clamp it, and cure in the heat box.

Rig the bow with the work string, sight along it to determine which recurve, if either, is out of line, and mark the edge that is pulling out. Unstring the bow and remove a small amount of material from the edge, smoothing it down to the recurve. Round the edges and refile the nocking notches. Restring the bow and check the alignment; repeat the operation as necessary to get the limbs straight, then

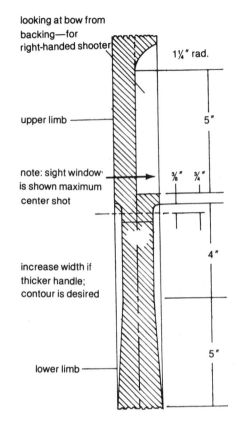

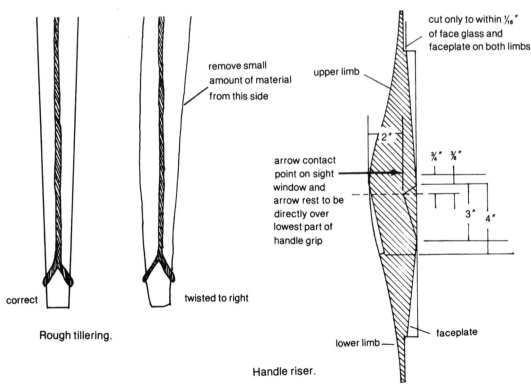

Rough tillering.

Handle riser.

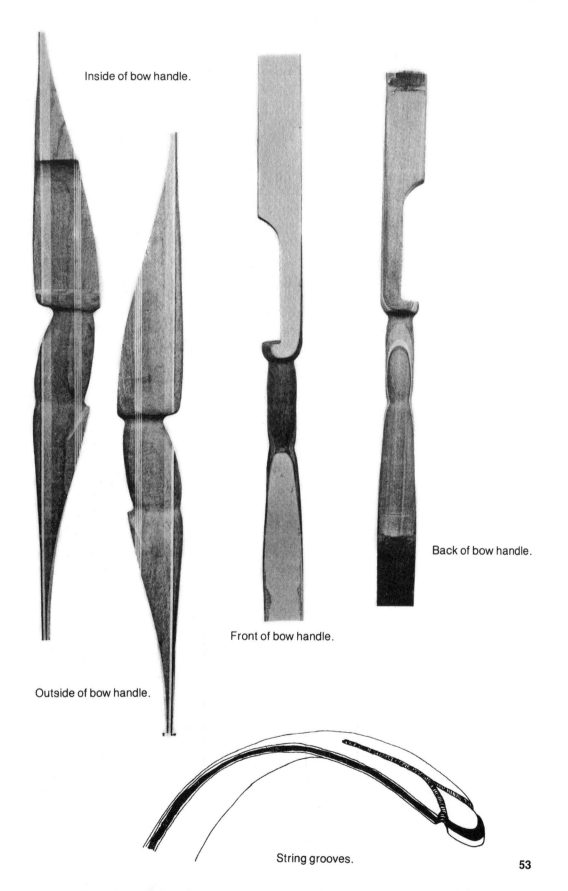

Inside of bow handle.

Outside of bow handle.

Front of bow handle.

Back of bow handle.

String grooves.

sight down the string to see if it is centered. If not, remove material from the wide side to center it. The string grooves in the nocking notches have to be absolutely straight across from each other, or else they will throw off the bow tip to one side or the other.

Remark the centerline on the riser and draw the shape of the handle on the masking tape, upper limb at the top. Cut the profile as shown and sculpt it to shape as shown. For the final "tillering," slowly reduce the width of each limb to bring tip weight down to minimum for maximum cast (speed at which arrow is thrown). This operation is done slowly, with frequent checking of the strung bow. Make a clean finished string with a straight height (measured from the bow handle) of 7 to 7½ inches. Work the string grooves down as shown.

Shoot the bow several times, then examine it for alignment. When it stays aligned, sand it smooth, then spray with a quality urethane gunstock finish.

BOWSTRINGS

You can also make your own bowstrings. Today's modern bowstrings are "endless" or of served loop design—simply loops of Dacron string wrapped around a form, tied together, wrapped on the ends to make the loop and on the middle for the nocking area.

You can drive spike nails into a 2 × 4 to hold the string loops, or you can make a bowstring jig for more effective and easier work. To build a bowstring, adjust the two end pegs so they are the exact distance apart you wish the bowstring length to be (standard bowstrings are normally 4 inches less than the length of the bow), or you can lay the old string on the jig if you're replacing an old one. Tie the Dacron bowstring thread to the post or nail and start winding around the two posts until you reach the number of strands required to give the necessary strength for your particular bow weight as shown.

You should use about 50 percent more turns when making up a work string.

Up to 35 pounds	10 strands
40 to 45 pounds	12 strands
45 to 50 pounds	14 strands
50 to 60 pounds	16 strands
60 to 70 pounds	18 strands
70 to 80 pounds	20 strands

Clip off the end of the string, untie the starting end from the post, and tie the two together. Now rotate the strands around the pegs until the knot is about ¾-inch in from one of the pegs as shown.

Using a dark crayon, mark the lengths you wish the loops to be on each end. Make the mark ¼-inch longer than the finished loop should be, and rotate the string around the pegs until the marked areas of the loops are in the center of the form board. Pull one side over the spreader loop and out of the way; now you're ready to "serve" or wrap one of the loops, which is done with ordinary heavy-duty cotton thread. It's much easier to make neat wraps if you use a simple bobbin made of a piece of heavy-duty wire and a long bolt through the thread spool.

Wax the string between the marks first with stringmakers wax, then start winding serving thread around the strings, keeping the serving neat and tight. Twist twice for extra strength. Tie with a fisherman's blind knot, then rotate string around pegs until you can serve around the other end loop. Rotate string back into position with loops around the end pegs. The ends should be offset about ¼-inch from the loop by tying the strings together in the same manner, serving the loop about 6 inches down on the string. Repeat the process on the opposite end, then remove the string from the right-hand peg, twist clockwise for a dozen turns, and replace back on the peg. Mark about 4 inches from either side of the center of the string, apply wax, and serve this area. As a final step, apply a tiny bit of model-makers' cement to the ends of the servings.

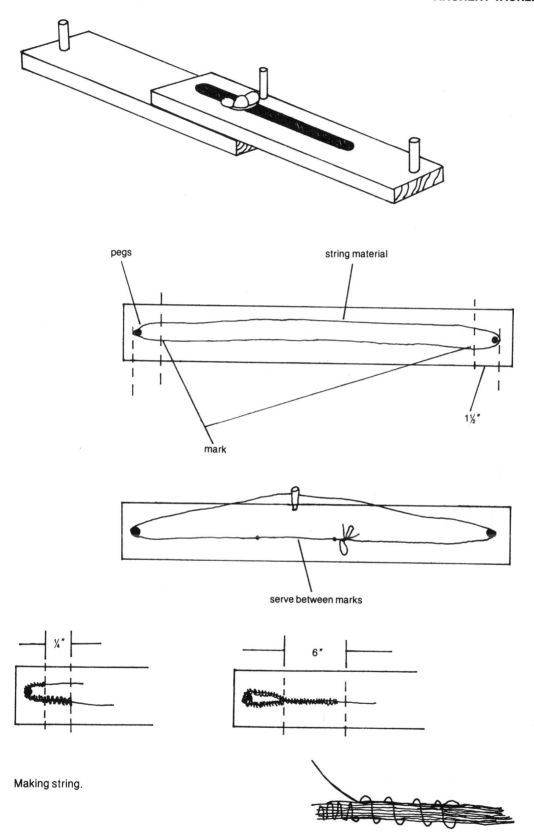

pegs

string material

mark

1½"

serve between marks

¼"

6"

Making string.

Caution: Never attempt to use a string that is too short; you may break the bow or cause injury to yourself or someone else.

ARROWS

Good arrows are even more important than the bow. They must be properly made so they will fly straight and true once they're released from the bow. On the other hand, making arrows is much simpler than making a bow, but it does require careful attention to details.

Just as in making the bow, the first-time arrowmaker should use a kit of arrows until he gets the hang of building them; then it's easy to graduate to making them from individually selected materials. The kits available have matched spines in the weight you need, with fletchings and points, just as you need. They're available in wood, fiberglass, aluminum, and carbon or graphite shafts. The equipment needed for making arrows is specialized, but like the bowmaking equipment, once you have it you can use it over and over to make as many arrows as you wish.

The tools needed are a fletching jig, dipping tank (you can make your own), feather trimmer, and a taper cutter. You may also wish to make up a cresting lathe and other items as you get more involved in making arrows.

It is extremely important that the arrow shafts have the correct "spine"—the stiffness of the arrow—which should match the draw weight of your bow. Most shafts are spined at the factory, so when buying blanks, make sure you purchase those spined to suit your bow. Specify the length of the arrow you will make, the weight of the bow, and the weight of the points desired. Once you have the correct shafts, you're ready to start.

Wooden Shafts

The first step is to taper one end of the shaft for the nock. This should be done using a nock-tapering tool (resembles a small pencil sharpener). Don't use a pencil sharpener, however, as the angle won't be correct and the nock won't fit properly or securely. You can use a belt sander, or even whittle the end if desired, final shaping it with sandpaper. The angle should be 22 degrees.

Place a nock over the tapered end of the shafts, but don't glue them in place. Measure the proper arrow length, from the bottom of the slot in the nock, allowing for the extra length the point will cover (on broadheads this is normally about 1 inch). Cut all arrows to this length using a fine-tooth saw, such as a hacksaw or coping saw, making sure you don't splinter out any of the ends. If you plan to use broadheads, taper the end using a broadhead taper cutter or sandpaper to 10 degrees. If you're using slipover field points, leave as is for now.

The arrows are painted by dipping in a good grade of automotive finish or lacquer. You can use a purchased dipping tank, or simply cut a piece of plastic piping to 36 inches and cement an end cap over it. The dipping lacquer should be as thin as possible, but still cover the blanks in two coats. Grasp the blank with a clothespin and dip it down in the tank twice, drying between each dip. Switch ends for the last dip. Go over it with fine steel wool to eliminate dust and raised slivers of grain.

Examine the end of the blank to determine the direction of the grain. Place a bit of fletching cement on the end of the shaft and push the nock in place so the nock slot is positioned across the grain of the wood. Carefully remove any excess glue. To apply the slipover points, first gently scrape away the paint, apply a bit of fletching cement to the end of the shaft, and push the point in place. You can fasten points in place by use of a knurling tool (use an old copper tubing cutter), or by making three indentations around the side of the point with a nail set and hammer.

Broadheads are glued in position using hot-melt Fer-l-tite cement. To use, heat ce-

Place nock over tapered end, measure arrow, and cut to the correct length with a hacksaw or other fine-toothed saw.

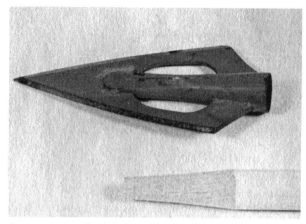

If arrows are to be broadheads, cut taper on end for broadhead, again using special cutter. If arrows are to be field points, leave end square.

ment stick and then smear on end of the shaft. Heat the arrow point, holding with pliers, warm the cement on end of the shaft, and push the point in place when cement starts to bubble. Align the point properly and remove excess cement. Since this type of glue hardens quite rapidly, it must be worked fairly fast. Stand the arrow up on its point and spin it with your hands while the glue is still warm. If the arrow wobbles, straighten the point until the arrow spins evenly. This is extremely important, as any point that is not straight with the shaft will cause the arrow to fly off course.

Single-blade broadheads are normally placed so they will lie horizontally when the arrow is placed on the bow rest. This prevents wind from affecting them in flight. Three blade heads should be placed with one blade down and the other two up in a V shape.

Dip arrows in automotive-type lacquer, at least two times to coat thoroughly. Use a dipping tank as shown, or make up one from a 36-inch piece of tubing.

Nocks and broadheads are glued in place, while field points are pushed over square end and crimped using a dull copper tubing cutter, or by punching slightly with a nail.

The cresting or colored bands on the arrows adds a final touch and also makes it easy to identify your arrows. These bands may be applied using a small brush, holding the arrow in a cradle as shown. Or you may wish to make up your own cresting machine as shown. For a neat job, keep the shaft rotating while applying the cresting, and keep the brush wet with paint so it flows well entirely around the shaft. By varying the size of the brush, you can change the pattern of the cresting.

The most important part of the arrow is proper installation of the fletching. It is impossible to get the feathers or vanes glued on in the correct position without a fletching jig. You can use die-cut feathers (already cut to shape), plastic vanes, or if you're a purist, full feathers and trim them with a fletching burner. The feathers used will come from both the right and the left wing of a turkey. Although it doesn't make any difference from which wing you use the feathers, all fletching on an arrow must be from the same wing. The size and shape fletching used is determined mostly by personal choice, but as a general rule you would use larger feathers on hunting arrows than on target arrows. Normally 5-inch fletchings would be used on hunting arrows while target arrows would use 3½-inch fletchings.

Set the fletching jig to the proper spiral—about 1/16 for target arrows and 1/8 for hunting arrows. Place the shaft in the fletching jig with the nock firmly seated. Put a thin bit of fletching cement on the cock (single-colored) feather and place it in position in the fletching jig and on the arrow. Don't allow the arrow or feather to move once you have positioned it. Apply the other two fletchings in the same manner and allow to dry for about thirty minutes.

If you use precut feathers you won't have to trim them; however, if you use full feathers

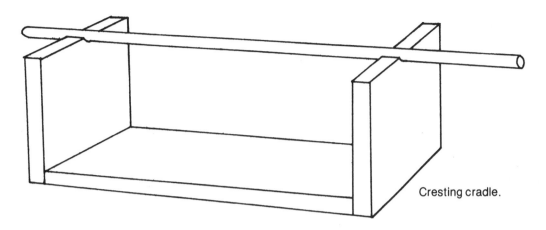

Cresting cradle.

Or make up a cresting machine, merely a cradle with a small geared-down motor used to turn the arrow while you hold the paint brush against it.

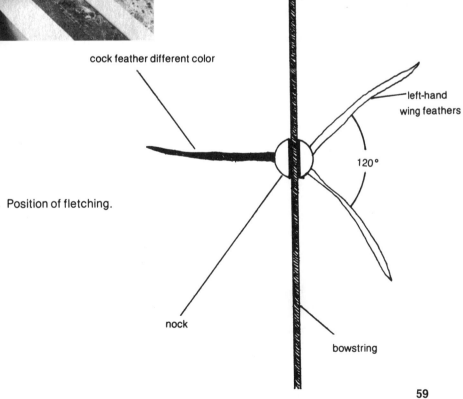

cock feather different color

left-hand wing feathers

120°

Position of fletching.

nock

bowstring

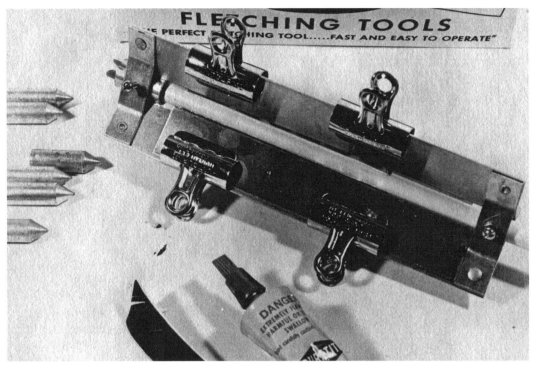

Fletching is glued in place using a clamp called a fletching jig.

To trim rough feathers to shape use a feather trimmer. This is an electrically heated wire which the feathers are turned against.

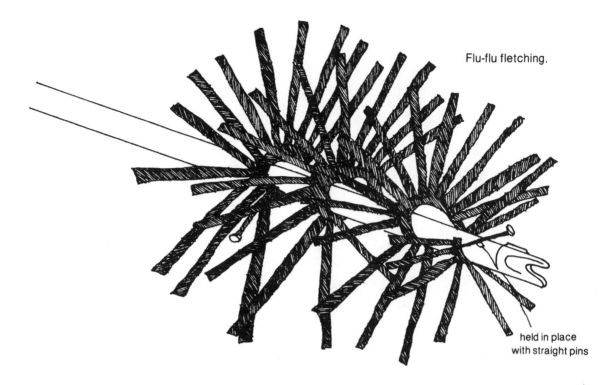

Flu-flu fletching.

held in place
with straight pins

they will have to be trimmed with a feather trimmer. This is nothing more than a thin wire heated to shape, and the feather turned against it. To use, turn on the device, allow the wire to get red hot, then simply rotate the arrow in the cradle, positioning the feathers down against the wire. Don't use force or you'll bend the fine wire out of shape.

For a last step, apply a good coat of paste wax to the arrows and check shafts for straightness.

If you wish to apply flu-flu fletching such as used at short ranges for birds and squirrels, use a full-length wraparound bushy type of feather. Glue in place in a spiral around the arrow, holding in place with straight pins. Leave approximately ⅜ inch between wraps.

Fiberglass Arrows

These come with hollow shafts and with the inserts for the nock and point either already fitted or not fitted. Cut to the proper length using a hacksaw, and file smooth. You must use epoxy cement to fasten the inserts in place. Fletchings are cemented on in the same manner.

Aluminum and Carbon or Graphite Arrows

The shafts are also hollow and the nock and point inserts are simply glued in place using a glue specified by the manufacturer of the shafts. To cut, use a fine-tooth hacksaw and file the ends perfectly square after making the cut.

THE BOW REEL

One of the best ways to extend your bowhunting fun is by making and using a bow reel. In the springtime when the carp and other rough fish move into the shallows in the lakes and river backwaters, you can really have a lot of fun, as well as filling your freezer with fine-tasting food.

One great way of expanding the hunting season is to make up a bow reel and hunt fish such as carp, buffalo, etc.

A bow reel is simple to make and simple to use. The one shown merely tapes to the bow with black plastic electrician's tape, and is quickly and easily installed and removed. String is wound on the reel and fastened to a fiberglass fishing arrow.

Making the bow reel requires the use of a lathe. The first step is to apply glue to two 6 × 6 × 1½-inch pieces. Then smear glue on one side of the glued-up block, place a piece of ordinary paper on the glue and smear one side of a 6 × 6 × ¾-inch block. Place the three glued-up pieces in a vise or set of clamps and clamp overnight until the glue sets. Make sure the wood pieces don't slip out of place before the glue sets.

After the glue has set, mark across the back of the blank (the ¾-inch piece) diagonally, from corner to corner to locate the center of the block. Position the lathe faceplate on the block and fasten it in place on the block with ½-inch wood screws.

Turn down the outside of the blank to the shape shown. Then position the lathe so you can reach the front of the blank. Turn down and hollow out the inside of the blank, gradually cutting down to the ¾-inch backing

Glue up the reel from two 6 × 6 × 1½-inch pieces. Then glue a third turning block on the back with a piece of paper sandwiched between.

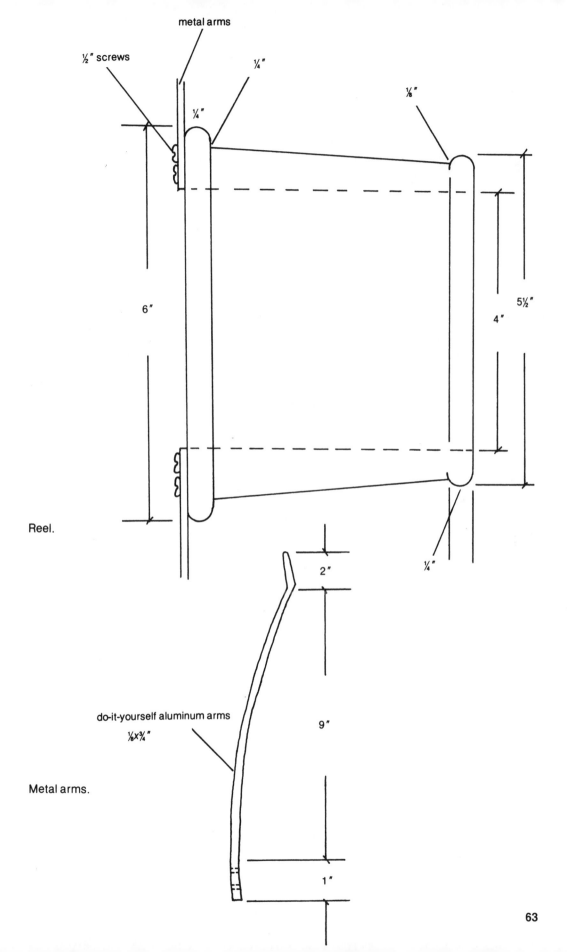

metal arms

½″ screws

¼″

¼″

⅛″

6″

5½″

4″

Reel.

2″

¼″

do-it-yourself aluminum arms
⅛×¾″

9″

Metal arms.

1″

Turn the outside of the reel down to shape.

Make the aluminum arms and fasten them to the back of the reel with screws.

Hollow out the inside down to the finished backing block, then use a sharp chisel to split the backing block away from the turning block on the paper line.

block. Smooth the inside and outside of the bow reel blank and apply several coats of polish while still on the lathe. Remove from the lathe. Using a wide, sharp chisel, tap gently at the paper line separating the turning block and the backing block. Tap all the way around the outside of the blank until the two pieces fall apart. Then sand and smooth down the back of the reel. Rub a bit of paste wax on it to seal the wood surface.

Cut two pieces of aluminum as shown. These are readily available at building-supply stores selling do-it-yourself aluminum materials. Drill the two holes in the ends of the aluminum strips, sand the edges and cut ends to knock down all sharp corners and edges (especially those that will be taped to the bow), and bend the aluminum to the proper angles by placing one end in a vise.

Now all that's left is to tie the string to the reel and wind it in place. Incidentally, a large

The reel is merely taped to the bow using black plastic electrician's tape.

rubber band cut from a bicycle inner tube will help hold the string in place during storage and while the bow is not actually in use.

To fasten the bow reel to the bow, position it in front of the bow so the center of the reel fits exactly over the center of the arrow rest. Then tape the two ends of the aluminum strips to the bow, using black plastic electrician's tape or any tape that will remove easily without leaving marks or material on the bow.

5

Fishing Rods

In days past, making your own rod meant gluing intricate pieces of bamboo together. This required a lot of knowledge, specialized tools and skills, plus time and patience. With today's hollow fiberglass and graphite rod blanks, almost anyone can create a highly decorative and beautiful rod, and it's a lot of fun to create your own fishing rod. You can also choose the rod blank, handle, and guides of your choice, and literally custom-build a rod to your exact specifications. Do you need a spinnerbait rod, a rod just for casting poppers to specs or redfish, or a flipping stick designed for your style of fishing? With the variety of rod blanks available you should have no trouble finding a rod blank as well as the other needed items. The rod blanks can be purchased separately or in kit form. Because the guides, tip and so forth are matched to a particular blank, you may wish to try one of the kits first. Later, you can go on to build your own rod from separate materials. You also may wish to modify the rods—for instance, make a blank shorter, make a two-piece rod from one single-piece blank, or

Rod making materials can be purchased in kit form, or individually.

make fly rods into casting and spinning rods for crappie "dipping."

ROD BLANKS

Most of today's rod blanks are made of graphite, or in some cases, fiberglass, and are hollow. These blanks are the same high quality you would get in a quality purchased rod. In fact, most companies sell brand name rod blanks from the most popular manufacturers. For instance, if you like All-Star rods, you can purchase an All-Star blank and custom build your own rod. It is important to understand the blank will have a different feel without the guides, wrapping, and handle. The addition of guides, wrapping, and handle has an effect on the overall action of the rod. As a result, rods that may have just the right action while in the blank may be a bit soft or "whippy" when all the weight of the fittings is applied.

In choosing the proper blank, you must know: 1. blank length; 2. ferrules supplied or not; 3. number of pieces; 4. weight; 5. action—stiff, light, etc.; 6. butt diameter; 7. tip diameter; 8. ferrule size; and 9. what type of handle it takes.

HANDLES

On casting rods the choice of handle styles is somewhat limited. However, many of today's fishermen are using the newer shaped flat grips rather than the old-fashioned straight-handled type. These soft contoured grips provide more leverage and take some of the effort and strain out of fighting heavy fish. In most cases, casting rod handles are fitted with a chuck. The rod blank is fitted down in the rod handle and the chuck tightened to hold the blank in place.

There is much more variety in spinning and fly rod handles. These are available assembled, or you can make your own. In either case, the rod blank goes almost all the way through the handle and is secured there by gluing the blank to the handle. Building your own handle to suit your particular grip is fun and naturally has advantages.

Both the spinning and fly rod handles utilize cork rings that are fastened over the rod

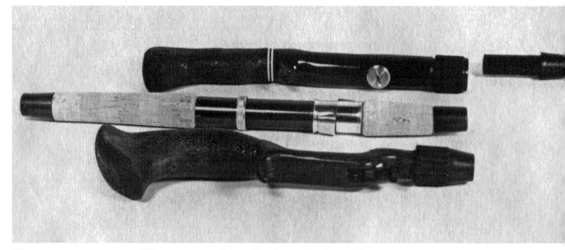

There are a great many different types of handles for rods, depending on what type of rod, size, etc. The casting rod handles at top and bottom of this photo have a "screw-down" chuck that holds the rod in place in the handle.

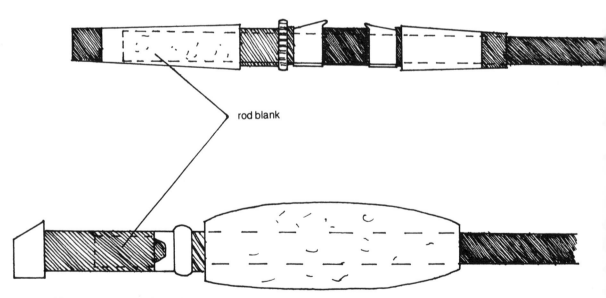

rod blank

Most spinning and fly rods have a "hollow handle." The rod blank goes completely through the handle. These handles are fastened in place by threading the pieces over the rod blank, then gluing the cork handle securely to the blank. The handles shown are "completed;" all that is required is that you slip the components over the rod blank and secure to the blank by gluing in place. You can purchase cork rings with center holes of the correct size to fit over rod blanks, or you can cut your own.

and glued in place. These are then shaped to suit. Both also utilize a metal reel seat placed over the shaped rings.

Installing the Handle

Installation of the handle is the first step in building a rod. If you are building your own handle, push the cork rings down over the rod blank, starting at the small end of the blank. If the openings in the rings are too small to allow the rings to slide down, open them a bit with a sharp knife or a piece of sandpaper on a wooden dowel. The rings should fit snugly, but if they are forced down over the blank they may break apart.

If you're building a fly rod, you can thread on all the corks; but if you're building a spinning rod handle, leave a few of the front

On the spinning rod handle shown, the front three cork rings that would "hold" the reel seat in place are left off until the reel seat is installed. This may also be the case on some fly rods. Then the reel seat area is "carved" using a rasp and sandpaper.

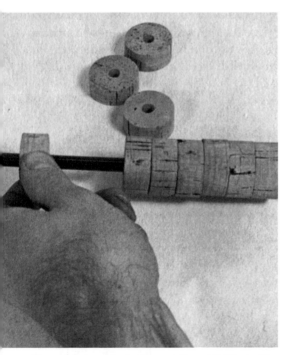

Thread the cork rings over the rod blank. You must be careful that you don't force the rings enough to break them or cause them to separate.

corks off at this time. With all corks in position, separate them a bit and force some marine or epoxy glue down between the cork rings and onto the handle portion of the blank. Push the corks back in position, wipe away all glue that has been squeezed out, and allow to dry until the glue has dried completely

Cut down the handle portion where the reel seat will be, using a wood rasp, and finally coarse sandpaper. The reel seat should fit snugly in place. On a fly rod the reel seat will be on the back of the rod; on a spinning rod it will be in the middle of the handle. When the reel seat fits properly, place it in position on the handle. On a fly rod you may wish to pin the reel seat in place by drilling a tiny hole through the end of the reel seat, down through the cork ring and rod blank,

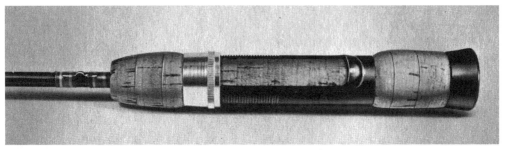

The reel seat is installed over the shaped cork, the three front rings glued in place, and remainder of handle shaped to suit.

making sure you're in the center of the rod blank. Then use a small piece of brass or copper wire or rod driven through the hole, peened over, and filed down smooth to hold the reel seat in place.

On a spinning rod you won't have to do this. Merely place a touch or two of epoxy glue on the reel seat corks, slide in place, and glue the front cork rings in place. This will hold the reel seat. Shape the remainder of the handle to suit. Add a butt cap glued in place with marine glue or epoxy.

APPLYING THE GRIP CHECK

A grip check is a small piece of plastic that fits over the blank and up against the front cork. It gives the rod a better appearance and prevents the front cork grip from becoming worn or damaged. It is merely slipped over the end of the blank and glued in place with hot ferrule cement. Any edges that protrude above the outline of the cork handle can be filed down to match.

GLUING ON THE FERRULES

In most cases the blank will come with the ferrules already attached to them, but if they don't or in case you wish to modify or change the rod, the ferrules are glued in place with

stick ferrule cement. Fit the ferrules over the rod pieces first to ensure that they fit properly. Then warm the ferrules with a candle flame. Melt a bit of ferrule cement from the end of the cement stick and rub it on the rod blank pieces. Push the ferrules over the ends and allow to sit for about thirty minutes. Clean away all excess cement before it sets; it is almost impossible to remove the cement after it has set up.

ROD WINDING

Winding on the guides is the place where you can really get creative. Choosing the proper set of guides is the most confusing part of rod building. There are literally hundreds of different kinds and sizes, and unless you are building the rod from a kit, there is just no way you can choose the correct size guides without some experimentation. Some of the equipment suppliers furnish guide kits for specific size rods and these might be the best to start with; otherwise you may have to purchase a complete set of guides and pick the right size and number after experimenting a bit with the blank. Incidentally, the least number of guides on a blank that will still do the job properly, the least amount of friction and the faster the rod will cast.

You will also need rod-winding thread. Read the manufacturer's specifications as to what sizes are offered and the amount needed for specific blanks. Normally this would be 60 to 85 yards for a medium-duty spinning or casting rod. This nylon thread is available in 50-yard and 100-yard spools in addition to bulk spools. It is available in all colors. Solid color threads are normally wrapped with one dominant wrapping and a finish wrapping of a contrasting color on the end. Or you can purchase thread that is "space dyed"—the thread is dyed in two contrasting colors spaced at equal intervals and by wrapping with this thread you end up with a banded wrap. Another type of thread is two-toned with contrasting colors of fibers woven into the thread. There are even fluorescent threads, and varigated threads (one thread dyed in as many as five different colors spaced equally). The rod you build and wind yourself can be as individual as your own personality, depending on your choice of thread and how you apply it.

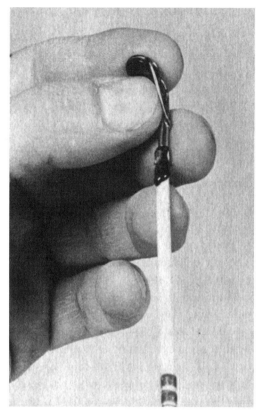

Fasten a reel on the handle and position the tip in place. Dry-fit tip first to ensure that it fits rod blank end properly. Heat rod tip (not tip of blank). Then place a coat of ferrule-cement on tip, and place a bit in the rod tip. Push tip in place, line up with reel on handle, and allow to set for about an hour.

GLUING ON THE TIP

Position the reel in place on the handle. After the reel is in position, glue on the rod tip. Check first to ensure that the tip will fit down over the rod blank tip. If it won't, sand just a tiny bit off the tip. It's easy to overdo it here, cutting way too much material and weakening the tip, so you might have to use the next larger size rod tip. In any case, make absolutely certain it fits properly before gluing it in place. The tip is glued on using ferrule cement. Heat the rod tip (not the blank) and melt a bit of ferrule cement using a flame from a candle. Push the tip down over the end of the blank and twist it around a couple of times to ensure that the cement is evenly spread around the tip. Turn the tip so it lines up properly with the reel, wipe away excess glue, and allow it to set thoroughly. This normally takes about an hour.

PREPARING THE GUIDES

In most cases the guides will be ready to use, but the guide feet may need to be filed a bit to enable them to fit down securely on the rod blank. On some guides the top of the foot may be rounded and will need to be filed down for a smoother wrap. Do not, however, make the point of the foot so sharp that it will cut into the rod blank and cause breakage or damage to the blank.

GUIDE SPACING

Probably the most important thing in rod building is proper spacing of the guides. If you purchase a kit, the instructions will show the proper spacing for each guide, but if you're building your rod from scratch you'll have to determine the guide spacing by trial and error.

Spinning Rods

With the reel fastened to the handle, measure from the front face of the reel spool to the tip of the rod and mark it into thirds. The first mark from the reel front is the approximate location of the first (largest) guide. Tape the guide in position at this point using masking tape. Don't use clear tape as it will leave a residue on the rod when it is removed. Run the line through the first guide, then thread the rest of the guides on the line allowing them to hang loosely. Run the line from the reel to the tip of the rod and tie it in position on the tip. Then tighten the line and hold it in position with a rubber band if necessary. The line must run from the bottom of the spool to the tip of the rod. Loosen the drag on the spool and rotate it several times to give you an

idea of the "cone" of travel of the line. Tape the next guide in position so that the line almost touches it on the down stroke. Again rotate the spool to ensure that the line doesn't touch at any time. (If you must move the guide a great distance, say 6 inches or more, you will need the next larger guide instead of the one you have on at that time.) Continue taping the rest of the guides in position in the same manner, making sure they don't touch the line and that they line up straight with the reel spool and the rod tip. If you have to compromise a bit do it at the tip section, not at the butt end of the rod.

Fly Rods

Establishing the guide distance on a fly rod is exactly the same procedure except the rod

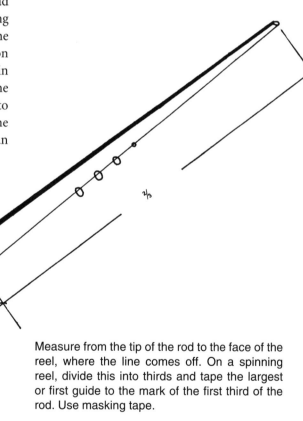

Measure from the tip of the rod to the face of the reel, where the line comes off. On a spinning reel, divide this into thirds and tape the largest or first guide to the mark of the first third of the rod. Use masking tape.

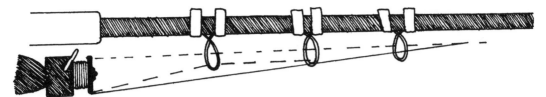

Run the line from the reel through the first guide, then through the rest of the guides, hanging them on the line. Tie the line to the rod tip. Place a rubber band or similar item over the reel to keep the line in place. Run the reel spool until line is at the bottom edge. Then move next largest guide in place so line almost touches but doesn't drag, then tape it in place and follow with rest of guides.

is divided into fourths instead of thirds and the first guide is positioned at the one-fourth mark. You should use a braced guide for the first guide. All the rest of the guides should be thin, wire "snake" guides to cut down on as much friction as possible.

Casting Rods

Casting rods have problems of their own. Use high-framed guides and again try not to choke down the line by using too small a first guide or too many guides. The biggest problem in casting rods is in creating a line gap or an area where the line can be pulled below the rod because of too widely spaced guides.

Locate the guides roughly on the blank and tape down. Tie a solid object to the line and pull the rod tip up slightly. Move the first guide so that it keeps the line off the rod, then continue placing the rest of the guides in the same manner. Turn the reel

several times to determine if the line is being choked sideways as it comes off the reel. Traditionally, small guides have been used on casting rods, but although they may look out of place, larger guides will give a faster cast.

For a final check of any kind of rod, secure the guides in place with tape, untie the line from the rod tip, run it out and tie to a heavy object on the floor. Bend the rod to see how the line fits the guides. Use the proper line test that matches the rod and be careful not to rip the guides out of the masking tape. The idea is that the line should follow the bend of the rod and not have any excessive angles through the guides. Sharp line angles will not only be hard on the guides, but in fighting heavy fish can actually cause the line to break at the guide.

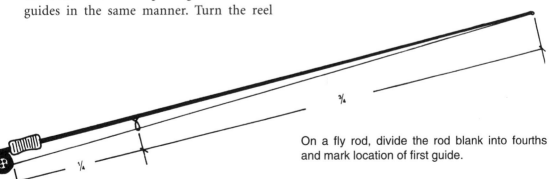

On a fly rod, divide the rod blank into fourths and mark location of first guide.

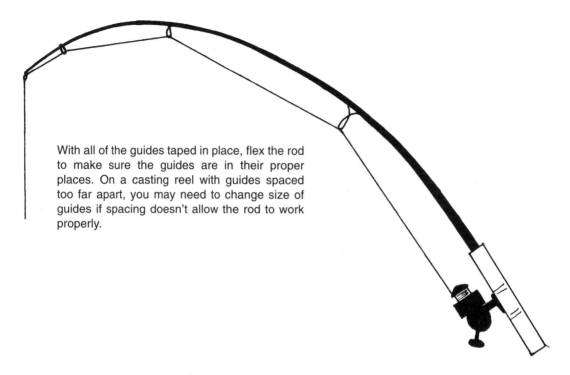

With all of the guides taped in place, flex the rod to make sure the guides are in their proper places. On a casting reel with guides spaced too far apart, you may need to change size of guides if spacing doesn't allow the rod to work properly.

ROD WINDING

With all guides properly spaced, you're ready for the actual winding or securing of the guides to the rod. This should be done on a flat surface. Make up a jig of a 1 ×6 piece of lumber about 2 feet long. Cut notches in the top edges to hold the blank in position. Because you will be using solvents and finishes, it is a good idea to place a piece of newspaper under the jig to catch the mess.

Place the rod in position in the cradle. The most important rule in achieving a good wrap is keeping the thread taut as it is wrapped around the rod. You can do this in two ways. First, make up a "bobbin" of a piece of wire shaped as shown. Place the wrapping spool in the bobbin and thread a small bolt through. By tightening the nut on the bolt, you can control the pull of the thread. A simpler method is to run the thread through the pages of a heavy book. You may wish to place

You'll need some sort of jig to hold the rod blank while winding on the thread for holding the guides in place. One of the best is simply a wooden cradle a couple of feet long made of a 1×6. Notches in the top hold the rod during winding procedure.

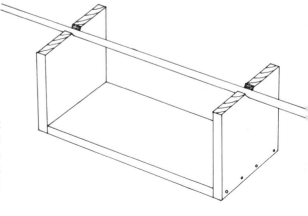

With all guides properly located, and rod blank in cradle, remove tape from one side of one of the guides. Start the thread wrapping. In this case wrapping is started next to guide. A "bobbin" made of a spool of rod wrapping thread, a piece of heavy wire, and a nut and bolt keep the thread taut.

In this case thread wrapping is started away from guide and brought to it. Thread is held taut by running it through the pages of a heavy book.

the thread spool in a small jar to keep it from rolling off the table.

Starting with the first, big, guide remove the tape from one foot. Using a felt-tip pen, mark the length of the wrap from the guide. You can either wrap from the guide out, or in toward the guide depending on your choice.

pull out enough line to lay over the rod blank and leave about 2 inches extra. Turn the rod so the thread coming out goes over the line and holds it securely. You may wish to tape this end of the line to the rod to get it out of the way. When the starting wrap is secure, turn the rod blank with your hand, rotating

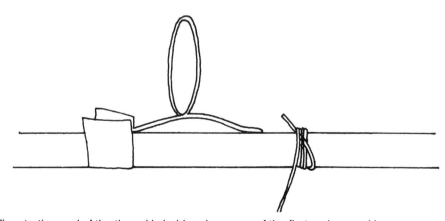

The starting end of the thread is held under wraps of the first and second loop.

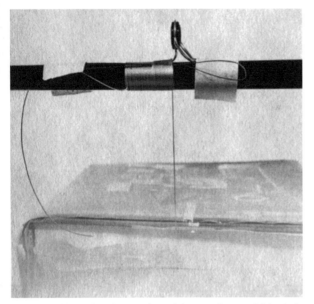

Wrapping is continued by turning rod blank in your hand against the thread. Keep thread wraps tightly on the rod and against each other. Place a loop of thread on the rod and continue the winding, wrapping over the thread loop.

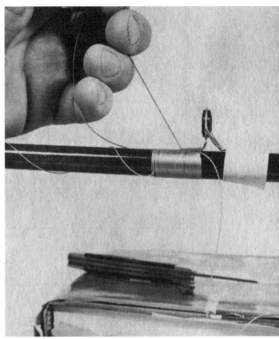

Clip off the wrapping thread, and holding it securely in place thread the end through the thread loop. Pull the end of the thread back under the loops.

the rod toward you and wrapping the thread around the rod. Keep the thread taut and the turns securely against each other as you turn the rod.

Wrap about two thirds of the winding in this manner, then lay a loop of thread on the rod and winding, with the loop headed away from the starting end. Continue to wrap the thread over the loop. When the wrapping is completed, clip off the end and slip it through the loop. Hold all portions of the thread tightly in place as you do this. Then pull the loop back under the winding, pulling the end of the wrap under as you do. Untape the beginning end and clip off both ends of the thread, or cut with a sharp razor. Make sure you don't nick any of the windings or pull the starting ends out as you cut them.

A main wrap may be decorated by wrapping a small contrasting band on the ends using the same techniques. Remove the tape from the opposite foot of the guide and wrap it as well. Then wrap the remaining guides in place. After all guides have been wrapped securely, sight down the rod blank and make sure that all guides line up properly with the reel and the rod tip. Any guides that are slightly out of line can be shifted back into position by pushing sideways.

You may wish to dress up the tip by wrapping about a half inch of winding in front of the tip, and even up over the tip edge on larger rods to provide more holding power.

COLOR PRESERVER

The purpose of the color preserver is not only to preserve the color of the windings but to cement the guides in place as well. Use a finish formulated just for that purpose. Use

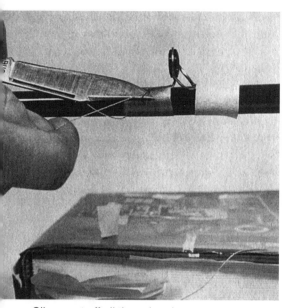

Clip or cut off all thread ends.

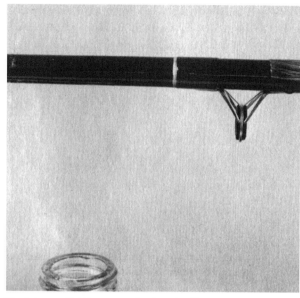

Push loops tightly up against each other.

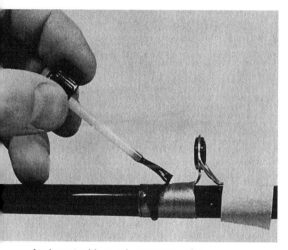

And coat with a color preservative.

Remove tape from opposite side of guide and wrap it in the same manner.

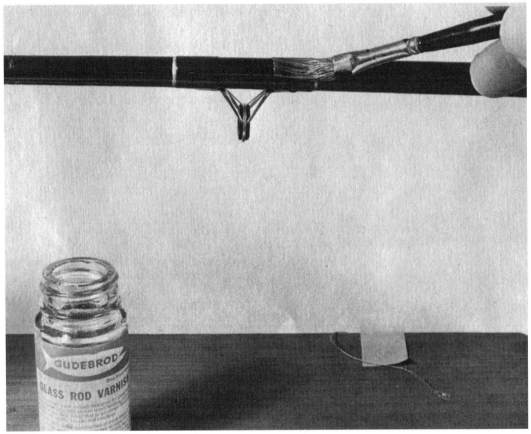

Apply the rod finish to the windings, coating them thoroughly with several coats.

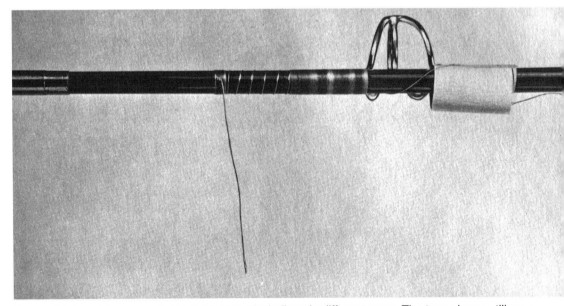

If you wish to get fancy, apply the guide thread windings in different ways. The type shown utilizes a varigated color thread. Other types are fluorescent-colored thread, using two different colors of thread to wrap in bands, and even two-toned thread.

the tip of your finger, or a small brush, to apply the color preserver to all portions of the winding, being careful to keep it off the bare rod. Wipe away any excess preserver with the tip of your finger. (Note: The color preserver will darken the windings when first applied, but the color will come back when the preserver has dried.) Let the preserver dry thoroughly, then apply at least three more coats allowing each to dry before applying the next.

The last step is to apply a rod finish over the windings after the color preserver has dried to protect the windings, add a bit more holding power, and keep water and dirt from the windings. The main thing in applying the finish is to get a good covering finish, but one that is smooth and even. Again it will take several coats, so apply thinly and evenly allowing each to dry thoroughly. The finish is applied to the windings only, not the rest of the rod.

If you wish to further customize the rod, give it a wrapping on the butt end next to the handle with "Butt Wind," a flat tape woven of thread. Wrap it in a spiral pattern out from the handle, then back, to give the appearance of diamonds on the handle. This is also given several protecting coats of color preserver, followed by rod finish.

6

Fishing Lures and Tackle

Fishing lures are probably one of man's oldest outdoor implements. Although today's ultramodern lures have come a long way from the first shell lures, they still operate on the same principle—either simulating the appearance of something to eat or getting the fish just plain mad, as in the case of an old largemouth bass.

There are literally thousands of different kinds and sizes of fishing lures, and indeed some of them are more adept at catching fishermen than fish. In addition to the few basic lures that have proven themselves over the years as consistent fish catchers, there are some relatively new ones that are also becoming welcome additions to the fisherman's tackle box. The best part about all lures is that you can easily make them yourself, not only saving money (some of the better lures cost up to $10), but also building a special shape or painting in a color that will suit your local area. A guide friend of mine down on famous Bull Shoals Lake in Arkansas uses a balsa wood model he hand carves. Then he paints it in the exact pattern of the perch from his area. He says they have a brighter orange belly

Making your own fishing lures can double the pleasure.

than normal perch and the bass seem to notice this in fishing plugs.

WOODEN PLUGS

When you mention lures, many people think immediately of wooden plugs made from balsa, cedar, or any other soft, even-grained wood. There are basically two ways of making wooden plugs—using two halves of balsa wood with a wire harness through the center to hold the hooks, or using a one-piece cedar or pine wood plug, fastening the hardware and hooks with screws.

Balsa Plugs

Most balsa wood plugs are made by first spot gluing two ¼-inch-thick pieces of balsa together. Don't smear the glue, or spread out over the entire piece. The idea is to glue the two pieces together temporarily, then separate them after the rough carving is done. Use a model airplane glue formulated for use with balsa wood. Position a book or other similar

Balsa wood lures are made by first spot gluing two pieces of the wood together with waterproof airplane glue. Then make a pattern using a 3 × 5 card or similar paper and trace onto the balsa wood blank.

weight on the blank to help clamp it in position until the glue sets. Allow the glue to set thoroughly before removing the glued-up wooden pieces.

Trace a pattern for the plug onto a 3 × 5 file card or other fairly stiff paper and cut to shape with sharp razor knife or scissors. Indicate what the pattern is on the paper and you can keep it indefinitely for making any number of the same kind of lure.

Position the pattern on the glued-up block and mark around the pattern with a felt-tip pen. Then cut away the waste with either a band saw, coping saw, or sharp knife. The lure can be rough-carved with a sharp pocketknife or special carving knife, whichever you prefer. When removing waste material, always make sure you go with the grain and keep turning the plug so you can keep it symmetrical. It's very easy to remove too much wood, and almost impossible to replace it, so go slowly and cut away material in small slivers or chunks. Balsa carves quite easily. In fact, you may wish to carve only the corners or sharp edges of the rough block, then remove the rest of the material with a medium-grit sandpaper. Again, remember to keep turning the small block to keep it symmetrical and make sure you don't take more off one side than the opposite. Smooth out any dents or rough edges with the sandpaper. Although this is to be only a rough shape of the lure, it should still be fairly close.

After rough carving, use a sharp knife to split the two halves apart. Mark the bottom of each so you can put them back together quickly and easily.

The hooks and eyes in balsa plugs are held in place by a wire harness running completely through the plug. Use a fine-gauge wire. Each plug requires a somewhat different harness configuration. These are bent using small needle nose pliers. One pair of small "full round nose" pliers will also help in making the end loops that form the tail and nose eyes. Bend

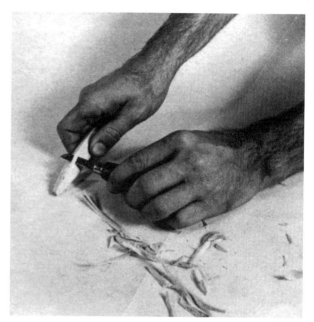

Using a sharp pocketknife or whittling knife such as shown (an X-Acto works fine), rough cut the plug to shape.

Basic outline can be cut on band saw, coping saw, or even whittled out using a sharp pocketknife.

the wire carefully to ensure that it will fit in the plug properly, then place it in position on the inside flat of the plug and mark with a felt-tip pen. You can also squeeze the two pieces over the harness to mark on both sides of the plug. Then remove and carve out the area on both plug sides to receive the harness.

With the plug-harness recess carved, smear both of the flat sides with model airplane glue. Place the wire harness in position between the two halves, making sure it is correctly placed, and squeeze the two halves together. You'll have to clamp the pieces together solidly. A small wooden clamp or small C-clamp works well for this. Or you can cut small strips of rubber from a bicycle inner tube and wrap around the plug to hold it together until the

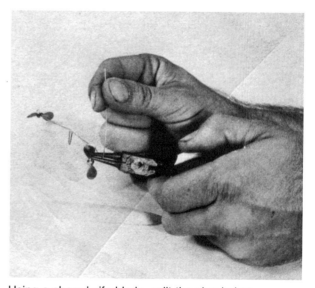

Using a sharp knife blade, split the plug halves apart and make up the wire harness. A pair of small full round nose pliers is the best for bending the loops, etc.

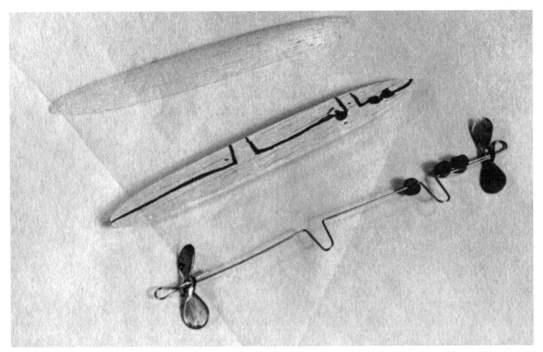

With harness complete, lay it in position on one half of the plug body and mark position. (Note, this plug has small split shot clamped to harness to weight plug into upright position in the water.) Carve out area in both sides of the plug body to accommodate the harness and weights.

Smear glue over both halves of body, then position harness in place and clamp halves together until glue dries. After glue dries, resand off glue and any rough spots using fine grit sandpaper.

glue sets. Examine the plug closely after clamping to make sure the wire harness hasn't slipped out of position, which happens quite easily. Also wipe away any excess glue you can reach with a small sharpened sliver of wood. Allow the glued-up plug to set completely, for at least four or five hours. Some glues and weather conditions may require that the plug be left in the clamps overnight.

Spoons or lips on plugs can be cut from ⅛-inch-thick stock. The trick is to take a block of white pine ¾-inch thick and however long the lip is to be (including that portion that must fit in the plug), stand the block on end and use a sharp chisel to split off a chunk about ⅛-inch thick. This can then be whittled, chiseled, or sanded down smooth. Cut a slot in the front of the lure for the lip. Make sure the lip fits in place perfectly and is true to the axis of the body. If the lip fits the plug crookedly, it will cause the plug to run to one side or may even cause it to roll completely over as you pull it through the water. Again, make sure you keep excess glue removed. Once dried it is extremely hard to remove from around the crevices and cracks of the lips.

After the glue has set thoroughly, the entire plug can be final shaped using medium- then fine-grit sandpaper. Again make sure you don't remove too much from one side. It's quite easy to do with balsa wood.

When the plug is shaped and sanded to suit, it is ready for the finish. There are many different kinds of finishes, depending on the particular type of plug, color pattern, and so forth. Plugs can be sprayed with a good waterproof finish from aerosol cans or they can be dipped in paints, and spots dabbed on with a small dowel. Or you can invest in a small air brush set, the kind that is used to paint model airplanes. These little sprayers are great for spraying small areas on plugs without having paint overlap into other areas.

A large cardboard box makes a good spray booth for spray paint and a piece of plumbers'

A large cardboard box provides a paint booth to spray paint the plugs. Use an enamel used for model airplanes or spray epoxy.

strap makes a handy hanger for holding wet plugs until the paint dries.

Regardless of which method is used, the first step is to coat the plug thoroughly with several coatings of a good waterproof finish. The easiest method is to dip the plug in white acrylic enamel. Allow to dry thoroughly and then use extra-fine steel wool or sandpaper to remove any raised slivers of wood. It's a good idea to repeat this operation a couple of times. The undercoat of finish shouldn't be too thick, and will probably need to be thinned just a bit to make sure it covers evenly.

If the plug is to be sprayed, follow the basic plug painting pattern shown. This is a stan-

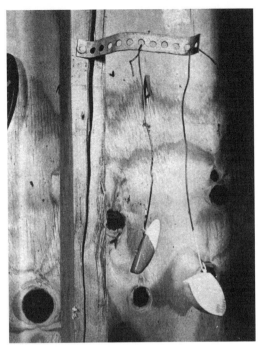

A short piece of plumber's strap makes an excellent hanger for freshly sprayed lures.

You can easily paint scale patterns on plugs as well. Make a small wooden frame and stretch netting fabric across it, holding it in place with thumb tacks or small strips of wood nailed down over the netting.

The first step is to spray the belly of the lure, then the sides, again with the lighter color. Lay the lure down with one side up, and position the netting frame down over and tightly against the side of the lure. Using a light dusting spray, paint a darker color over the lighter color. Or if you prefer you can reverse this and use dark on the undercoat and a lighter color on the top. My favorite method is to paint the belly white, the sides silver, then follow with black on the sides over the silver. Allow the first side to dry thoroughly and then spray the opposite side. When both have dried, position the plug in a straight up and down position on its belly, and spray the back of the plug.

To paint on eyes, use a dowel sharpened on the ends in a pencil sharpener and then dipped into enamel. For two-color eyes, use two sizes of dowels and both a white and black color. You can also easily paint spots on lures in this manner. "Decal eyes" that are simply stuck on the lure can also be purchased. Then paint in the mouth or any other features. Finally spray with several coats of clear epoxy enamel and allow to dry.

Some plugs are dipped instead of sprayed. For instance, the popular two-color, red and

dard perch or bait fish pattern, and regardless of the colors used the shading pattern should be the same. Always start with the lightest color, spraying on the underside or belly first with white or yellow, using spray epoxy or the enamel used for model airplanes. Then proceed to the sides, and finally put the plug on its belly and spray the darker color on the back.

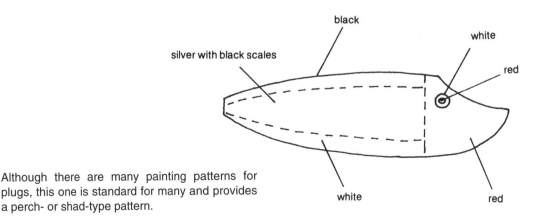

Although there are many painting patterns for plugs, this one is standard for many and provides a perch- or shad-type pattern.

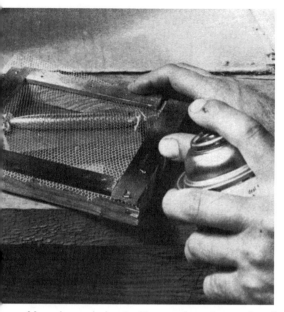

Many lures do best with a scale pattern painted on them.

The resulting pattern sprayed on a plug. For finer painting operations, a small air brush set such as that used by model airplane builders works best.

Some plugs are merely dipped in waterproof paint. This popular pattern is made by first dipping the plug in white paint, then dipping it in red paint holding it at an angle as shown.

The eyes are applied.

white plugs may be painted much easier by dipping. Solid color plugs and those with spots instead of scales are also easier to paint by dipping. The first step is to dip the plug into the white undercoating as before. After the plug finish is smooth, dip in white, this time using a full coat of paint. Allow to dry, then dip one end in the red paint, tilting the plug as shown. Apply the eyes as before. These plugs can be sprayed with epoxy finish or merely dipped in a good grade of marine varnish and left to dry. The marine varnish gives a much glossier appearance to the plugs, and you may wish to dip all plugs in the varnish for the final finish.

Cedar or Pine Plugs

Plugs can also be made from soft even-grained white pine or cedar. In fact, some of the most famous plugs are hand carved from cedar. One of the best places to get the cedar is from a couple of shake shingles that have the butts from ¼-to ⅜-inch thick. Split these and glue together to make the plug blanks.

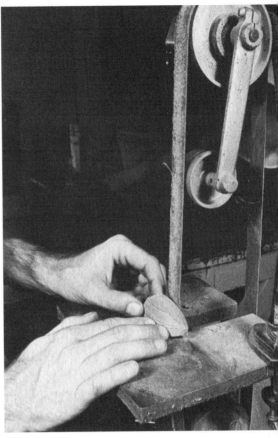

Or you can bandsaw them, then carve and sand them to shape.

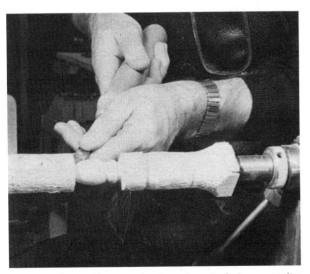

Some plugs are best made out of pine or cedar. Those that are shaped right can simply be turned on wood lathe.

Some plugs can be turned on a lathe, which makes it easy to mass produce these plugs in any quantity you desire. When you can make your own plugs for a few pennies, you don't become so alarmed at throwing them back into the weeds and brush.

The cedar or pine plugs are made in much the same manner as the balsa wood plugs, except they're made in one solid piece instead of two separate halves glued together. The hooks and hardware for these plugs are held in place with tiny screw eyes and screws. They may be band sawed, lathe turned, or whittled, but the basic finishing process is the same. Again, go slowly and

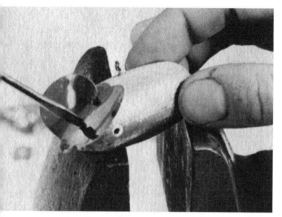

Purchased hardware for plugs is fastened in place with tiny screws.

Front lips may be epoxied in slits cut in plug, while others may be screwed in place.

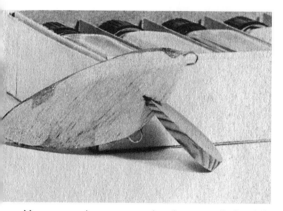

You can make your own hardware and glue it in place.

If you wish to get fancy, you can purchase eyes and install them in tiny drilled holes.

make sure you don't remove too much material at a time. Cedar or pine plugs are finished in exactly the same manner as the balsa wood plugs. The different types of metal hardware are available by mail order from numerous sporting-goods companies. You can also purchase kits that have plastic-bodied plugs ready for finishing and installing the hardware.

ALPHABET PLUGS

These easy to make, popular, and consistently effective "crank-bait" plugs are definitely ones to have in your tackle box; it's a good idea to have several of different colors. The balsa wood body allows the plug to float when at rest, yet when pulled under, the large turned-down lip immediately points the plug down. The faster you crank it the faster it dives, and the slimmed-down tail makes the plug wobble quite fast. The ⅛-inch-thick lip is made of white pine and is glued in a slot cut in the underside of the plug. Make sure the lip fits squarely with the body of the plug.

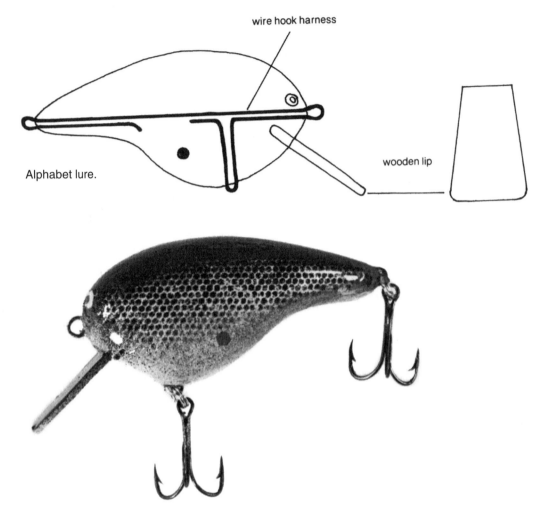

wire hook harness

Alphabet lure.

wooden lip

This popular alphabet plug is good in many colors. Lip is glued in slot. It's one of the most famous balsa wood lures.

CRAWDAD PLUGS

These are very good largemouth as well as smallmouth plugs. They should be made in two sizes, the larger one for largemouth bass and one about three-fourths the size for smallmouth. The large lip on the front (back) of the plug makes the plug dart down when pulled. This plug is made in the same manner as the alphabet plug, except the wire harness is weighted in the back (front) of the plug with three No. $\frac{1}{32}$-ounce-size split-shot weights. This makes the head of the plug drop down when cast, then pulling on the line makes the plug dart backwards in the nature of a real crawdad. The faster you pull this plug, the deeper it goes.

FLOATING MINNOWS

The original floating minnow lure was carved out of balsa. This is one of my favorite lures and it is also very easy to make. In fact,

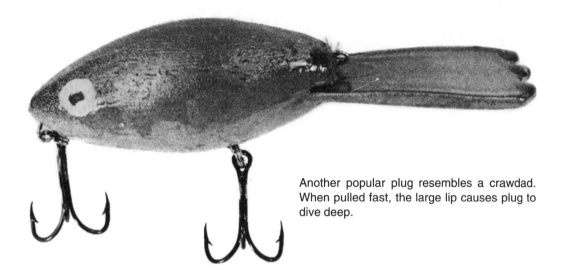

Another popular plug resembles a crawdad. When pulled fast, the large lip causes plug to dive deep.

it's a good idea to make several of the lures, painting them in two patterns, black and silver, and gold and dark brown. One resembles a shad and the other a perch, both good bait fish patterns. Make them in different sizes and you will probably find the size that works best in your particular area. Again the lip is cut from a sliver of white pine and glued in a slot cut in the bottom of the plug. To work

the plug, cast it into a spot, allow it to sit for a minute, then gently twitch. Allow to sit still again, then reel it in in steady slight jerks. Usually fish hit on the first jerk as you start to reel it in, or just before the plug reaches the bank or boat.

You can also make these floating minnows fat, like the alphabet plugs, and put spinners on front and back for a crippled minnow ef-

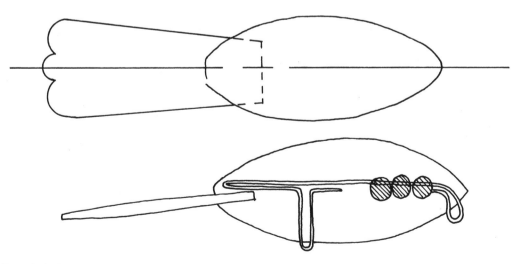

Crawdad plug.

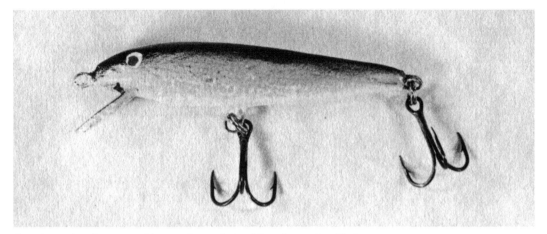

A surface plug that resembles a minnow is traditionally made of balsa.

fect, as well as cutting them in half and joining the two halves with a wire hinge for a jointed minnow. The variety of this particular type is endless, and all will catch fish. They're great for large lakes, small ponds, and even tiny streams.

CRIPPLED MINNOW PLUGS

Greatly resembling the floating minnow in shape, the crippled minnow is nothing more than a torpedo-shaped balsa wood plug. Propellers on both ends kick up a fuss when the plug is retrieved. To make the plug even more effective, place a couple of No. ⅟₃₂-ounce-size split-shot weights on the harness at the back of the plug. This will cause the plug to rest with its rear end submerged in the water. A slight twitch of the line will cause the lure to lurch forward creating a burble and fuss with the spinners on both front and back.

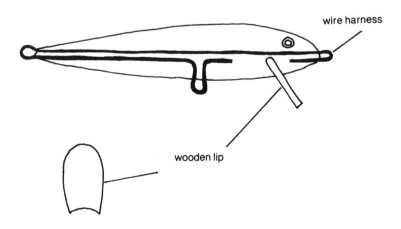

Minnow plug.

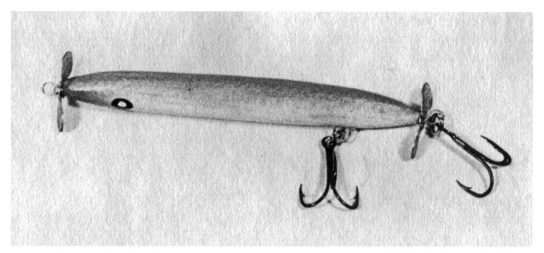

One of my favorite topwater plugs is this crippled minnow plug. Weights in bottom end cause plug to stand upright in water. Jerking it causes propellers to spin and it really kicks up a commotion.

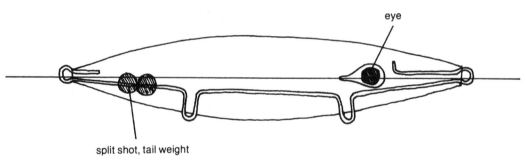

Crippled minnow plug.

LOUISIANA PLUGS

These famous plugs from the bayous of Louisiana are traditionally carved from cedar. They are best painted white or silver with a blue spot around the eye. The plug is tapered both from front to back and from top to bottom. It can easily be cut with a band saw for the outline, then the tapered portion carved. The hooks are anchored with screw eyes. The screw eye for the line is anchored in the very top of the plug, giving it a fantastic wobbling action when pulled through the water.

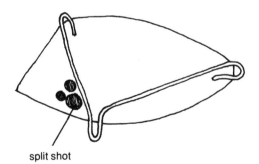

Louisiana plug.

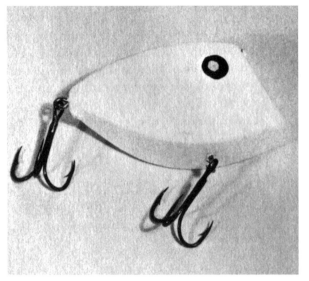

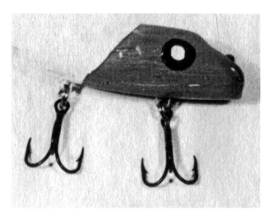

Another all-time topwater lure for bass fishermen is this one. It is best painted in a white and red pattern.

This famous Louisiana plug is made of cedar and made to resemble a shad. It is traditionally painted white or light blue.

them in scale patterns, and they are excellent in the yellow, orange, gold, and brown pattern of perch.

FLOATING DARTERS

These popular floating plugs can be made of balsa or pine. If you make them of pine you can turn them on a lathe, then scoop out the front portion by whittling. I prefer mine made of balsa because it gives them a much more subtle action; just a gentle twitch causes the plug to dart and dip slightly underwater. The traditional color of white and red makes them effective as bass plugs. You can also make

BANANA PLUGS

Good for anything from musky to trout, depending on size, these plugs are also one of the hardest to carve properly. If done correctly, they will wobble when retrieved even at slow speeds; if not carved evenly, they will have a tendency to run off to one side. They can be made either from balsa with an inside wire harness or of solid pine or cedar with screw-on hardware.

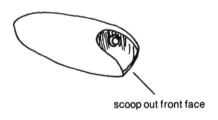

scoop out front face

Floating darter.

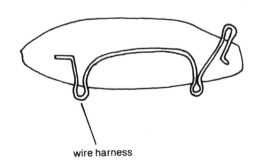

wire harness

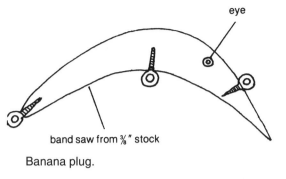

Banana plug.

This topwater plug wobbles and gurgles as it is jerked across the top of the water. The front scoop made of metal is purchased.

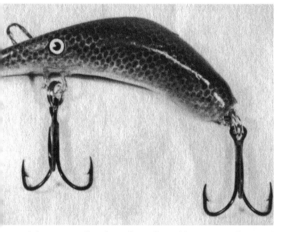

A banana plug is a favorite with many pike and walleye fishermen.

TOPWATER WOBBLERS

A great surface lure, the topwater wobbler is simply a sausage-shaped lure made of cedar. The metal lip that causes the plug to wobble is held in place on the scooped-out front with tiny screws. These wobblers can also be easily mass produced on a wood lathe. And it's a good idea to have several colors, although the spotted frog pattern is the most popular. A solid black works well for night fishing.

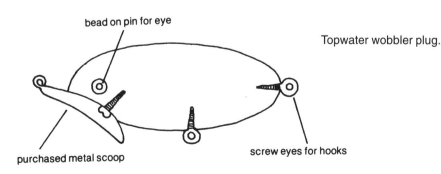

Topwater wobbler plug.

95

SURFACE POPPERS

Another old favorite, these cedar or pine plugs can be turned on a lathe. The scooped-out face makes a distinct popping sound when the plug is jerked through the water.

Topwater plug with an open mouth and skirt is another old-time bassing plug.

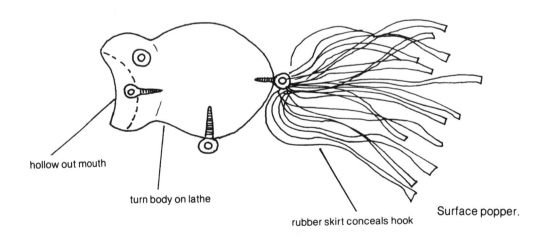

hollow out mouth

turn body on lathe

rubber skirt conceals hook

Surface popper.

SURFACE DARTERS

Simple and easy to make, these dependable plugs will dart under the surface and stay a few inches when retrieved.

THIN SHADS

A popular plug on the larger lakes, the thin shad is made from a single ¼-inch-thick piece of cedar or pine. The lip is extra large and causes the lure to dive and wobble. In areas where there are a lot of shad baitfish, it is especially good finished in silver and white with a blue back.

RIVER DARTERS

One of the oldest patterns, these are good plugs to have in your tackle box. The easiest way to make them is to turn them on a lathe, then scoop out both sides of the face. You can also make them of balsa.

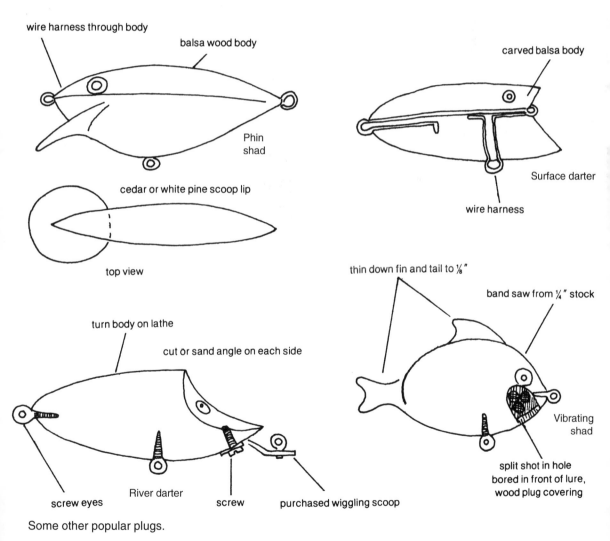

Some other popular plugs.

VIBRATING SHADS

Similar to the shad lure above, the vibrating shad gives off a definite vibrating action when retrieved.

KIT LURES

If you don't wish to go to the trouble of hand carving your own lures, yet you still would like to finish your own, you can purchase kits of plastic lure bodies. You merely glue the two halves together, finish as you wish, and screw hardware in place. It's rather more economical than buying finished plugs.

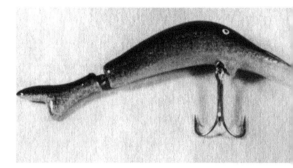

All you have to do is finish them and install the hooks.

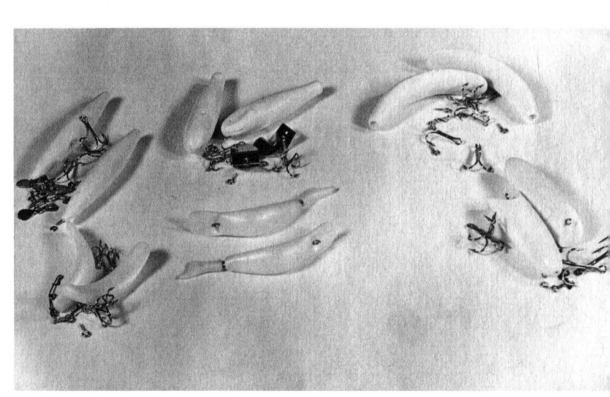

If you don't wish to make up your own lure bodies, you can purchase them in plastic shells as shown.

JIGS

Jigs are one of the easiest and most economical fishing lures to make. And it's a good thing they are, because to be fished right, whether they're tiny crappie jigs, or large jigs for bass, you'll use a lot of them. You can make and tie the exact kind and color you desire. Regardless of what type or size jig you plan to make, the basic process is the same: pour the jig from lead, tie on dressing, and paint head.

You will need a torch, a ladle or something else to melt lead in, hooks, and a jig mold of the type jig you desire to make. You will also need jig hooks of the proper size, fly-tying

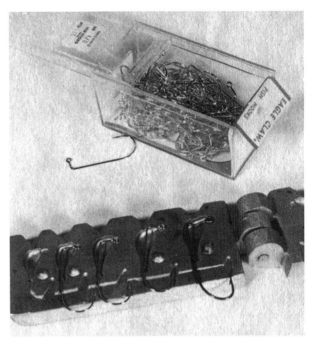

Select proper size hook and insert into jig mold.

Jigs are also great fishing lures. All you need are hooks, a jig mold, lead, feathers, paint, and tying thread.

thread, lure paint, and either bucktail, marabou, or whatever else you wish to dress the jigs with.

The first step is to open the jig mold and insert the proper size hooks on it. Then close the mold, place a rubber band around the handles or place the mold in a vise to hold it, and keep the mold closed during the lead-pouring process.

Place small chunks of lead in a melting pot or cast iron ladle (small chunks melt faster, so cut chunks of lead into small equal sizes). You can get scrap lead in many places, but the two most likely are tire repair shops and garages. The lead wheelweights on automobiles make great jigs. You can also purchase lead by the pound from plumbing supply houses.

Using a torch or other heat source, heat the lead until it is molten. Don't apply the heat directly to the lead, you'll only melt portions of it on top and will scorch the lead. The lead will also be unevenly heated, and when you

begin to pour it in the mold, it may set up before you can get it poured. Instead, heat the container holding the lead. My favorite method is to place the handle of the ladle in a vise and heat the bottom of the ladle until the lead melts. The heated ladle keeps the lead hot and molten during the pouring process. Use heavy-duty leather gloves, and eye protection, and take all safety precautions when melting and pouring the lead. Molten lead is dangerous and can cause a bad burn if spilled on you. You should also be careful not to breathe the fumes, as the fumes from melting lead can be poisonous.

When pouring the lead into the mold, pour in a single, smooth pour. It takes a bit of practice to pour perfect shaped jigs, but the lead can merely be reheated and reused again if you don't come out with good ones the first time. Allow the lead and mold to cool thoroughly, then open and remove the jigs.

Some jig molds have a place for weed guards to be attached, others do not. You can easily make room for them by routing a

Melt lead in a ladle or pot and pour into mold. Mold is held in vise.

Open mold and allow jigs to cool, then remove.

tiny "sprue" or channel in the mold with a portable electric grinder. These weed guards are nothing more than a bundle of pieces of heavy-duty monofilament placed in the channel before pouring the lead. The melted lead holds the mono weed guard in place. Touching the end of the mono weed guard with a burning match will melt all pieces of mono together, making it easier to hold them.

You will notice that the jig bodies have a large funnel-shaped piece of lead at the front, plus a thin edge all around. This is the sprue and flashing and must be trimmed off with a sharp knife or a file. Then use a smooth file or medium-grit sandpaper to smooth down all edges of the jig. This takes only a few minutes, but makes all the difference in whether the jig hangs up on brush or not.

Position the jig securely in a vise and place the feathers or hair on the back of the jig. Tie securely in place with fly-tying

Place feathers or hair in place on jig and tie with thread. Continue wrapping body of jig with thread, then tie off.

Trim flashing off jig head with sharp knife, then cut off sprue as shown here.

thread. Continue wrapping with thread until the hair or feathers are securely wrapped and held in place. Then tie off with several half hitches, pulling snugly in place. Using lure enamel, paint the wrappings, then clip off the thread and excess feathers. Paint the jig head in the same color or a different color as the thread. The jig heads may easily be painted by merely dipping in paint and hanging up to dry. Then if you wish, paint eyes on them with a sharpened dowel and punch out the paint filling the eye of the hook.

Always clean out the eye of the hook on all the lures you make. Nothing is more exasperating than trying to get the paint out of a hook eye when the fish are biting and you're in a hurry to get the lure tied on.

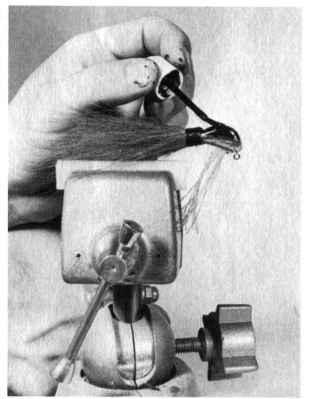

Painting the jig head.

SAFETY PIN LURES

Among the most popular types of lures today for largemouth bass are the safety-pin-type spinner baits. They come in all sizes, shapes, and colors and, in fact, are quite easy to custom build. Although you can purchase the mold to pour the lead or jig portion of the spinners, you can easily make your own mold from a couple of pieces of hard, even-grained wood. Use your favorite type and size spinner as a pattern and draw around it on a block of wood. Then use a small portable hand grinder to remove a channel for the hook holding wire, and lead-head portion. Do this equally to the two pieces of wood needed to make up your mold, and cut a sprue or lead-pouring hole in the shape of a funnel from the top of the mold, again on both sides. Incidentally, you can also make your own weight molds, jig molds, etc., in this manner.

After building the mold, make sure both pieces of the mold are evenly carved, then

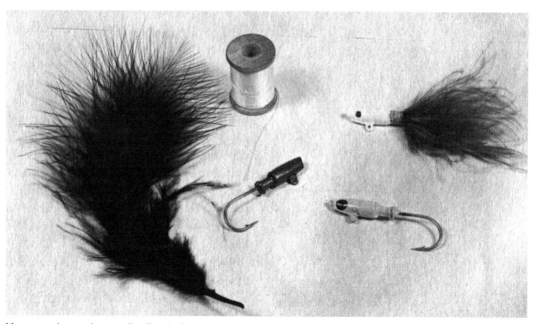

You can also make smaller jigs in the same manner.

Some jigs with pork rinds.

fasten a 6-inch piece of .030-inch-diameter wire to the hook with a small eye as shown. Place the hook and wire in the mold and clamp the two pieces together in a vise. Melt the lead and pour in the top sprue hole. Allow the lead to cool and remove the poured lead head from the mold. Again, remove the sprue and cut away any excess flashing or lead from around the lure body. Although the wooden mold may scorch, you'll find you can pour a couple dozen lures before it will be necessary to make another one. Dip or paint the lure body with a quality epoxy lure paint and allow to dry. Then use a pair of round nose pliers, bending the rest of the wire to shape and position the correct spinner blades, spacers, and beads in place. Push the plastic skirt over the hook portion of the molded body and you're in business. You may wish to reverse the process if you have wire lengths with preformed ends; install hardware, spinners, spacer beads, bend wire, then mold lead head.

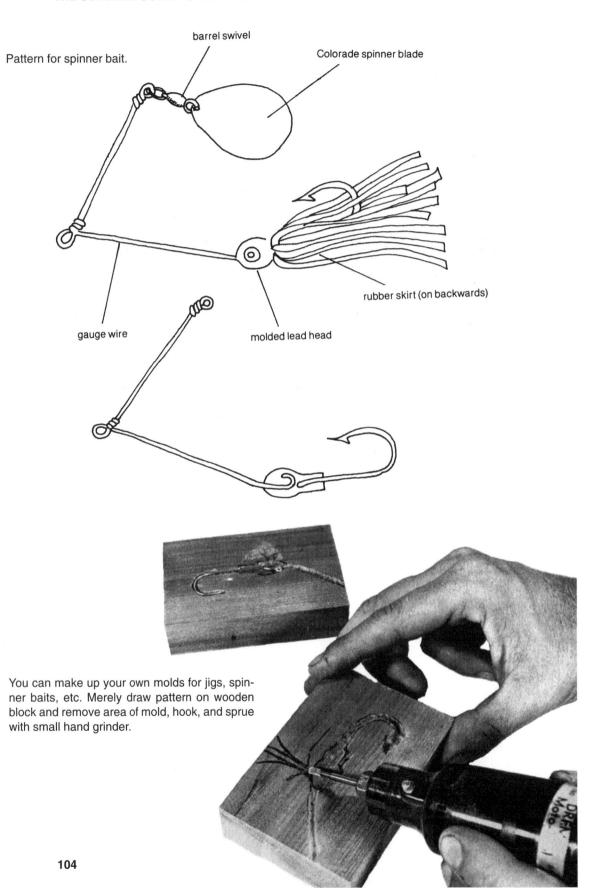

Pattern for spinner bait.

barrel swivel

Colorade spinner blade

rubber skirt (on backwards)

gauge wire

molded lead head

You can make up your own molds for jigs, spinner baits, etc. Merely draw pattern on wooden block and remove area of mold, hook, and sprue with small hand grinder.

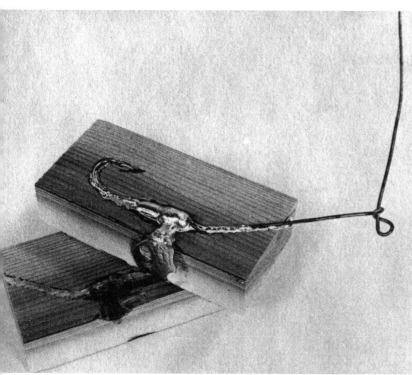

Then pour with lead.

Using round nose pliers bend wire to right shape and install spinners.

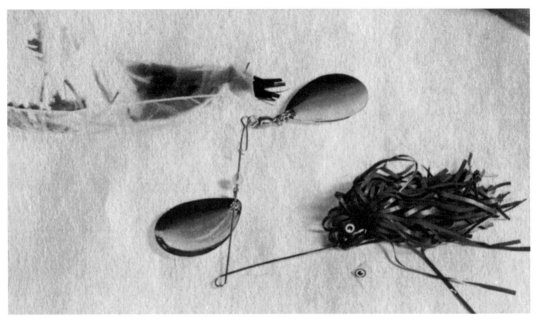

Finished safety-pin spinner. Eyes are "decals."

SMALL SPINNERS

Probably the most versatile of lures are the small spinners. They can be used for fishing for anything from trout to musky, depending on size, shape, and coloring. They're made by merely forming a loop in fine piano wire, stringing on the correct beads, metal bodies, and spinners, then making another loop and installing hooks and dressing. All parts to make up the different lures are available from mail-order sporting-goods dealers, and you can purchase parts to make up duplicates of all the most popular style lures.

The hard part is forming the wire loops or eyes, but this is easy if you have a wire former, a small inexpensive device that can be used to quickly form wire loops. This is used by merely inserting the wire in the end, forming a sort of hook over the turning hook, then pushing the holding lever down in place. By turning the crank you can form eyes, then thread on the parts you desire and turn the eye on the opposite end. The hooks are held in place by the use of split rings.

The bodies as well as the spinner blades may be painted in the colors you wish. Good colors for the blades are red and white or black with yellow spots.

PLASTIC WORMS

Molds and the plastic to bake your own plastic worms in your oven can be purchased, but an even better way is to use the bits and pieces of old plastic worms that have sifted down to the bottom of your tackle box.

The first step is to pour a bit of plaster of paris into a small cardboard box, then using your favorite worm as a pattern, push it halfway down in the plaster of paris and allow to set. After the plaster of paris has set, smear petroleum jelly over the first half of the mold and pour plaster of paris over the mold and worm, making a complete two-part mold. Allow the mold to set, then remove from the cardboard box, take the two

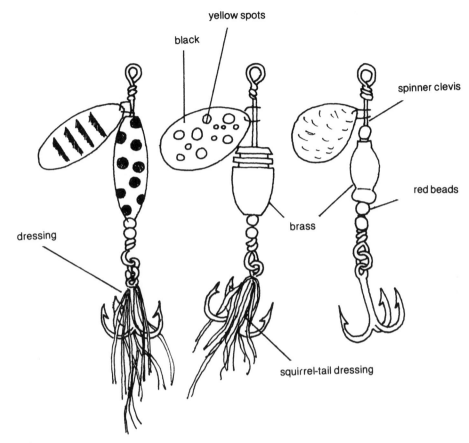

Various spinners.

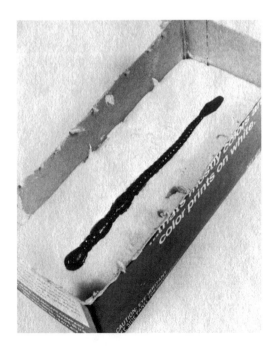

You can make your own recycled plastic worms. Pour plaster of paris in small cardboard box and push worm down into plaster.

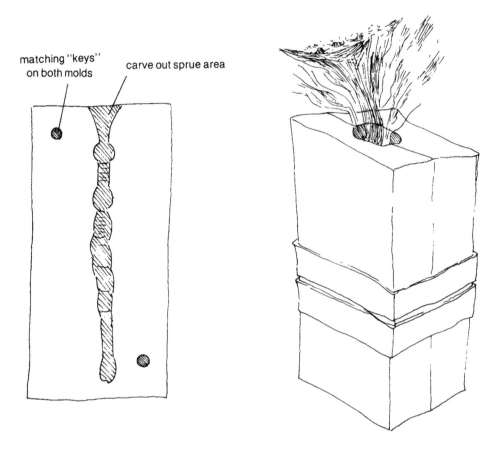

matching "keys"
on both molds

carve out sprue area

Allow plaster to set, smear with petroleum jelly, and then pour second half of mold. When cured, separate mold halves, cut a sprue opening in top and clamp together with rubber bands.

mold halves apart, and remove the original plastic worm.

Like the lead molds, you'll have to cut a sprue hole in the top, so clamp the mold halves together with a heavy-duty rubber band and cut a hole down from one side with a sharp pocketknife.

Place bits and pieces of plastic worms in a double-boiler arrangement on the kitchen stove, melt and skim off dirt and debris from the top of the liquid, then pour in sprue hole. When the liquid has cooled, remove the rubber bands and take the two mold halves apart.

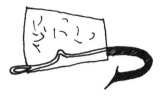

1. Slit cork, place hook in slit, glue in place using model airplane glue

2. carve cork to shape

3. make eyes with beads and cut off straight pins

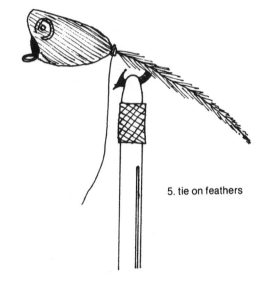

5. tie on feathers

4. dip cork body in paint, then spot paint on the eyes, etc.

You can make your own poppers using cork bodies, hair, feathers, and hooks.

WEIGHTS

Making your own fishing weights is easy using the proper molds. Merely melt lead and pour into the molds, allow to cool and re- move the weights. In fact, if you do very much bait fishing, making your own weights is the only way to go.

It's easy to pour your own weights using mold shown.

7

Sportsman's Storage and Workbenches

HUNTER'S CABINET

Guns, ammo, clothes, flashlights, calls, binoculars—it doesn't take long for hunters to acquire a lot of gear. Proper storage is a necessity, not only for safety of the guns and ammunition, but also to protect your investment. The cabinet shown is designed to fit in a garage with a standard 8-foot ceiling. It's well over 7½ feet tall inside, offering lots of space, even for bags of decoys, guns, and clothing.

The cabinet shown is constructed of ¾-inch fir "good" or "sanded one side" plywood. The back can be ¼-inch particle board or plywood. The shelves are of ¾-inch plywood or particle board. The cabinet can be made "fancier" if desired for placement in a den or "sporting room" by constructing it of oak or birch plywood or to match other cabinets. Note the cabinet is made to fit an 8-foot ceiling with just a little to spare. Measure your ceiling before beginning construction and adjust the height if necessary.

Ceiling-high storage cabinet holds a large amount of hunting gear. Has lock for safety.

Guns, ammo, clothing, gear, and even bulky items such as decoy bags are easily stored in this cabinet.

Construction

Because the cabinet fits so tightly against the ceiling it must be constructed in place, and requires some unusual construction methods. First cut the sides to the correct width and length from a 4 × 8 foot sheet of plywood. The easiest method of doing this is to place the plywood on two sawhorses, with a ¾-inch block of wood under each corner. Set the blade of a portable circular saw to cut just through the plywood, but not deep enough to cut down into the sawhorses. Measure and snap a chalk line, or use a straightedge to determine the cut. Cut down the middle of the line. As you reach the end of the cut, hold up on the board to prevent binding of the saw blade.

Once the pieces are cut to width, cut them to the proper length. Then place another 4 × 8 foot sheet of plywood on the sawhorses and

Materials List
A. Sides; ¾ plywood × 24 × 94½", 2 reqd.
B. Top; ¾ plywood × 24 × 46½", 1 reqd.
C. Bottom; ¾ plywood × 24 × 46½", 1 reqd.
D. Doors; ¾ plywood × 24 × 94¼", 2 reqd.
E. Inside divider; ¾ plywood × 24 × 93", 1 reqd.
F. Back; ¼ plywood × 48 × 94½", 1 reqd.
G. Shelves; ¾ plywood × 16 × 22½", cut to fit, 3 reqd., or to suit.
H. Divider support strips; ¾ × ¾ × 24", 2 reqd.
I. Top shelf support strips; ¾ × 1½ × 24", 2 reqd.
J. Closet pole; 22½", cut to fit, 1 reqd.
K. Gun rack; ¾ × 3 × 22", 1 reqd.
L. Gun rack back support; ¾ × 2 × 22", 1 reqd.
M. Gun holding strip; ¾ × 3 × 22", 1 reqd.
Hardware
Closet pole brackets; 1 reqd.
Hinges; as required.
Door handles; 2 reqd.
Door latch; 1 reqd.
Magnetic catches; 4 reqd.
Adjustable shelf strips; 48", 4 reqd.
Shelf brackets; 8 reqd., or to suit.
No. 8 × 2" self-starting wood screws.
No. 8 × 1¼" self-starting wood screws.

Cordless portable tools such as the Makita jigsaw make it easy to construct the cabinet.

rip this in half as well. This produces the center divider, top and bottom. Cut all these pieces to the proper length.

With the major pieces cut to the correct length and width, stand one side piece up on edge. Either get a helper at this point or prop the piece in place with a sawhorse. Stand the top up and position it against the side. Fasten in place with No. 8 × 2-inch self-starting wood screws. Make sure you keep the screws aligned and that they don't come out through either the inside or outside of the plywood facing. Repeat this step with the bottom. Measure and mark the location of the top and bottom divider support strips. Rip the strips to size using a rip fence and a portable circular saw or with a table saw. Fasten in place with 1¼-inch self-starting wood screws.

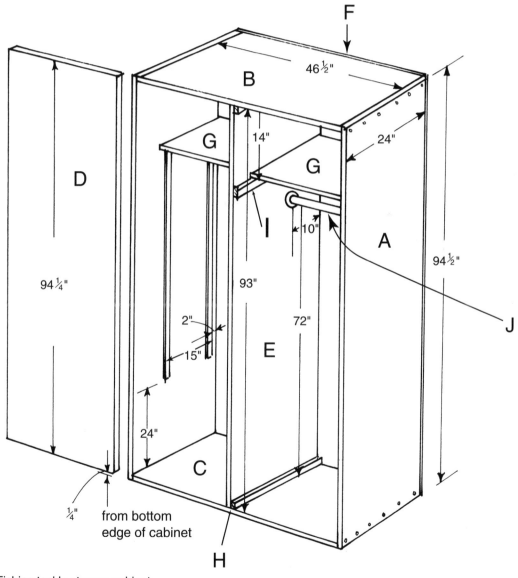

Fishing tackle storage cabinet.

Now for the hard part. Turn the assembly over on the side with the top and bottom standing up. Grasp the cabinet assembly at the top end and stand it up. The top piece will bend down as it's pushed against the ceiling, but the screws will support it temporarily. Another person can help a great deal at this time. Once the cabinet is stood upright, push the top piece back up and slide the divider in place between the top and bottom and against the support strips. Make sure it meets the top and bottom front and back edges properly then fasten in place with 1¼-inch self-starting wood screws.

Position the opposite side in place and fasten with 2-inch self-starting wood screws. Finally place the back against the back edges of the top, bottom, and sides, making sure the cabinet is square. Use a carpenter's square and align all edges, then fasten in place with 1¼-inch self-starting wood screws.

Install the closet pole. Rip the top shelf supports from ¾-inch solid stock and fasten in place with 1¼-inch self-starting wood screws.

The other side space utilizes shelf brackets for adjustable shelving, plus a gun rack that holds seven guns. Fasten the shelf brackets in place, installing their tops 6 inches from the inside of the case top on the gun rack side. Then cut the shelves to fit between. Cut the gun rack, using a jigsaw to make the circular cutouts. Fasten the back rack support strip to the gun rack with 1¼-inch self-starting wood screws. Place the top shelf at the top of the shelf supports. Then measure your longest gun and position the bottom gun holding shelf on the shelf supports with enough space for your guns between the two shelves. Place the gun holding strip (for the gun butts to rest on) on the bottom shelf, but do not fasten. Hold one of your guns in place and position the top gun rack in place so the gun is held away from the cabinet back. Check to make sure the scope is not resting against the cabinet back. Make sure there is proper spacing from the shelf to the top rack to hold all your guns, then anchor both the rack and gun holding strip in place with 1¼-inch self-starting wood screws. Note, there is ample room behind the gun butts for several boxes of ammo.

The final step is to cut and hinge the doors. Note the doors are set up ¼-inch from the

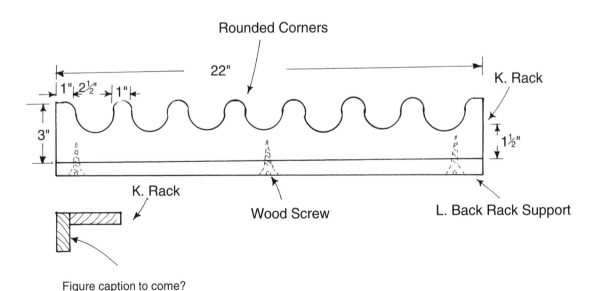

Figure caption to come?

bottom of the cabinet. Concealed hinges were installed on this cabinet, however, butt hinges or even piano hinges could also be utilized. The doors are fairly heavy and require stout hinges or several hinges to a side. Magnetic catches were added to the top and bottom of each door to keep the large door from warping. We also installed a locking door latch. Although not burglar or child-proof, it is a help. A key-lock hasp could also be used. Install desired hardware. Purchased cabinet door racks can be added to the inside of the cabinet doors. A variety of these are available from your local building supply. A strip with shelf hooks can also be added to hold calls on lanyards, caps, etc. The cabinet can be painted, stained, and varnished or given a clear coat of finish. You might also wish to glue a felt strip to the gun rack to protect your gun barrels from scratches.

FISHING CABINET

Most of us have organized our boats with specific places for rods, tackle, raincoats, safety equipment and other necessities like food. "Everything in its place" makes the boat easier and safer to operate and makes fishing more fun and productive. When it comes to the garage, however, it's often a mess with rods stacked in a corner, tackle boxes stacked here and there and clothes just about anywhere. The fishing cabinet shown solves the problem of garage chaos. The design, adapted from the hunter's cabinet, is well over 7½ feet tall inside, offering storage space for even 7½ foot flipping sticks as well as tackle and clothing. If you're an avid hunter and fisherman, you may want to add both cabinets to your garage.

The fishing cabinet is constructed using the same materials as the hunter's cabinet and is constructed in the same manner except only shelves are installed in one side and items K, L and M from the materials list are not used.

Berkley vertical rod racks are installed inside the doors and with two of these racks installed, the cabinet will hold 12 rods. Arrange the shelves to suit for tackle storage, electronics, or other fishing gear.

RELOADING BENCH

Like many hobbies, reloading is easy and fun if you have the proper equipment and place to work. The first requirement is a sturdy bench to hold the reloading tools and supplies. For safety, and ease of use, the bench should be solid and wobble free. You may in fact, wish to bolt the bench to the wall or floor. The latter can be done using angle irons.

The height of the bench is important. If you prefer to work seated, the bench should be at table height of 20 to 30 inches. If you prefer to work standing or from a higher stool, the best height is 36 to 38 inches. The bench shown is designed for use while standing or seated on a stool. You can adjust to a seated bench or to your stature by simply making the legs shorter or longer.

Good materials are necessary in order to create a sturdy bench. Soft, easily split woods with knots or other defects can weaken the bench. The bench shown was created using some scrap, pressure-treated 2 × 4s the author had on hand from a corral building project. Pressure treated materials are not necessary, but they tend to be better grade and stronger than the white pine dimension materials most commonly found in building supply yards. Yellow pine is also a good wood, with oak the best, although the latter is quite expensive. The top is made of ¾-inch plywood in order to provide a smooth working surface.

The use of self-starting screws not only makes construction easy, but results in a very sturdy project. The bench can be constructed with only a few tools; a handsaw, drill with bits as well as screwdriver bits, carpenter's square, tape measure, and straightedge. A heavy-duty

Ceiling-height fishing storage cabinet holds 7½-foot rods, clothing, tackle, and lots of gear. The Berkley vertical rod racks hold 12 rods, 6 rods on the inside of each door.

24-volt cordless power tools make assembly easy.

A sturdy bench makes reloading easy, safe, and fun and you can build it quite easily.

cordless drill, such as the Craftsman Industrial ½-inch 18.0 volt drill/driver, coupled with their Speed Lok accessory, makes the chore quick and easy. The Speed Lok features a chuck resembling an air chuck that fits into the electric drill. A drill bit with a shank fitting the chuck is snapped into the Speed Lok, and holes are predrilled for the screws to prevent splitting out the wood. The drill is snapped out and the power driver snapped in place. The Power Driver has a sliding exterior and is magnetized to hold the screw until it is started. Fastening is quick and easy.

Construction

Measure and cut all legs and support pieces to the proper length, making sure the cuts are square. Lay two legs on a smooth, flat surface

and position the top side support piece across them, extending the ends of the support piece past each leg 1½ inches. Drive one screw in each end of the support piece. Use the carpenter's square to assure the assembly is square and drive two more screws in each end of the top support piece.

Position the bottom side support piece in place, 6 inches up from the bottom of the legs and with the back end also extending past the legs 1½ inches. Fasten in place with three screws in each end. Fasten together the opposite leg assembly in the same manner.

Lean one leg assembly against a wall or table and position the top back support board on it and against the end of the end top support. Position the opposite end of the top back support on the other leg assembly. Drive one screw in each end. A helper can certainly

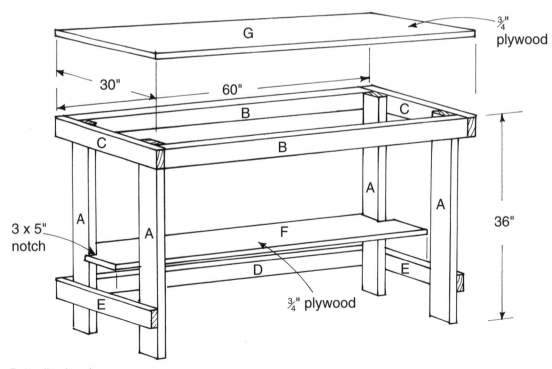

Reloading bench.

make this chore easier. Use a carpenter's square to make sure the assembly is square and drive two more screws in each end of the top support into the legs and two screws from the side top supports into the top back support. Position the back bottom support in place and fasten in place in the same manner. Turn the assembly over and fasten the front top support in place in the same manner. Note there is no lower front support.

Turn the assembly upright and measure for the bottom shelf. Cut the bottom shelf from ¾-inch plywood, and cut notches for the legs in the rear of the bottom shelf. Fit the shelf in place and anchor with screws into the lower back and side supports using the No. 8 × 1½-inch screws.

Cut the top to size and position it down on the assembly. Make sure the assembly is square and anchor the top in place using the

No. 8 × 1½ -inch screws. The screws should be just slightly countersunk, or level with the top.

A coat of paint or clear finish can be applied to protect the bench.

Materials List
A. Legs; 2 × 4 × 36", 4 reqd.
B. Top back and front supports; 2 × 4 × 57", 2 reqd.
C. Top side supports; 2 × 4 × 30", 2 reqd.
D. Back bottom support; 2 × 4 × 57", 1 reqd.
E. Side bottom supports; 2 × 4 × 28½", 2 reqd.
F. Bottom shelf; 3/4" plywood, 18 × 60", 1 reqd.
G. Top; ¾" plywood, 30 × 60", 1 reqd.
Self-starting screws; No. 8 × 2½", 40 reqd.
Self-starting screws; No. 8 × 1½", 40 reqd.

FISHING TACKLE WORKBENCH

Winding line on your reel, repairing a reel, sharpening hooks, sorting tackle, and

Angler's workbench provides a comfortable place to fill reels with line, work on reels, sharpen hooks, change hooks on lures, and other angling chores.

numerous other angling chores are made much easier with a good, solid workbench. Fishing bench shown is built exactly like the reloading bench and uses the same materials. Again, the bench height can be changed to suit. The bench size allows you to place it against a garage wall and still leaves plenty of room for your vehicle and/or boat. The bench features a smooth, flat top and a shelf on the bottom for tackle boxes and other gear. The bench shown is plain, without accessories other than a line spool holder above it which consists of a board with wooden dowels glued in it. Top supporting drawers can also be added beneath the top and they're available in the closet organization section of most large building supply stores. Small organizer bins can also be added to the top to hold split ring pliers, spare hooks, and other gear and tools.

8

Decoys

Decoy making is a valuable American folk art. Decoys were used by the first Americans, and are still being used by today's waterfowl hunters. A good set of "deks" is probably the most important equipment a waterfowler can own. Making your own decoys is challenging and practical. You can make decoys to suit your particular type of hunting, and at the same time have higher quality decoys at a lesser cost. Today there is also a great demand for decorative decoys, those decoys destined never to see the icy wind or gray water of a storm-tossed bay, but instead to grace the coffee table of a collector. Carvers who achieve any competence at all have no trouble finding a market for these decoys.

Decoys have been made from just about everything: bark, corn shucks, clumps of mud, wood, cork, pieces of driftwood. Today many of the mass-produced decoys are made of hollow plastic. Granted they are much lighter in weight and quite durable, but gunning over a set of decoys you hand carved yourself gives you a good idea of what the heritage of waterfowling is, as well as the warm satisfaction in creating your "hunting."

Making your own decoys is fun, practical, and a great way of spending the idle, winter months.

The most durable kind of decoy you can make is an old-fashioned wooden one. By choosing the proper wood and hollowing out the inside, you can keep the weight problem to a minimum. Early wooden decoys were made from many objects, especially discarded pieces of old ships and white cedar poles carefully cut from the swamps and cured just right. White cedar is still one of the most durable, water-resistant woods. It is also light in weight, takes a finish good, and carves beautifully. If you can't get white cedar you can use basswood, or white pine, as long as there is no "wild grain" in it.

The first step after choosing the wood is to enlarge the squared drawing for the decoys you choose. Make a template from heavy paper and transfer it to the wood blocks. The heads of all decoys shown can be made from a 2×4. The bodies are made of a glued-up block of wood with the center block hollow as shown. Cut the hollow block from two pieces of wood, or use a drill and saber saw to cut out the center portion of one block. A saber

saw, coping saw, or band saw can be used to rough-cut the heads and bodies to shape. Make sure you follow the outline carefully.

The glue used should be waterproof. A good marine glue or resorcinol glue found at any building supply dealer will do. Make sure the tops and bottoms of all the blocks are smooth, and clamp securely overnight until the glue sets up solidly.

Now comes the fun part, the rough shaping of the decoy. To help keep the decoy evenly carved, mark a line down the center of both the head and body blocks with a felt-tip pen. By using the centerline as a reference, you can keep from carving too much off one side.

The heads can be carved with a sharp pocketknife or carving knife; merely whittle away the excess amounts of wood until a rough shape forms. Use small wood rasps for the final roughing-in of the head. Another handy tool is a small, portable hand-held grinder. These, fitted with metal burrs, will quickly cut away excess wood, and the variety of cutter shapes available enables you to reach into

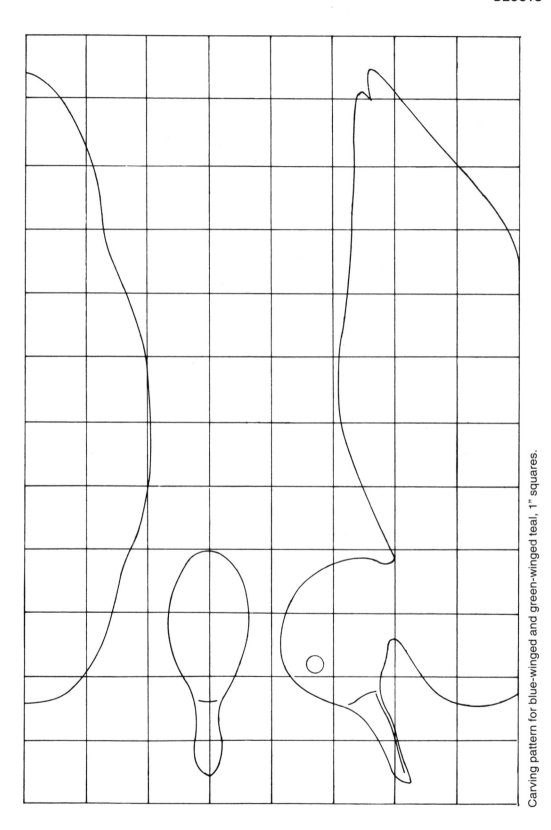

Carving pattern for blue-winged and green-winged teal, 1" squares.

Carving pattern for mallard, pintail, widgeon, etc. Use same body pattern, change the head.

1" squares

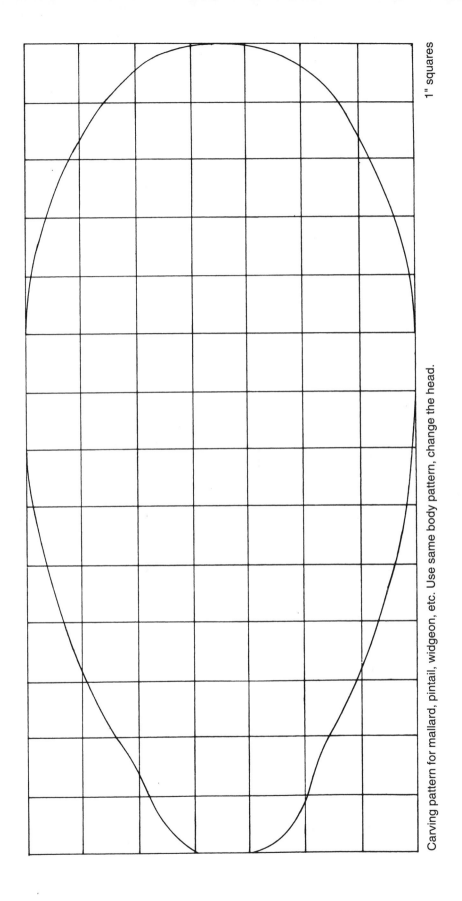

Carving pattern for mallard, pintail, widgeon, etc. Use same body pattern, change the head.

1" squares

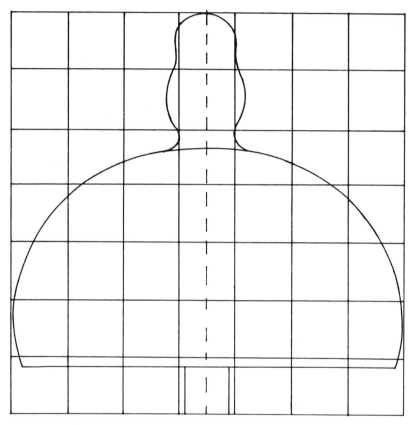

1″ squares

Mallard head pattern. Carving pattern for mallard, pintail, widgeon, etc. Use same body pattern, change the head.

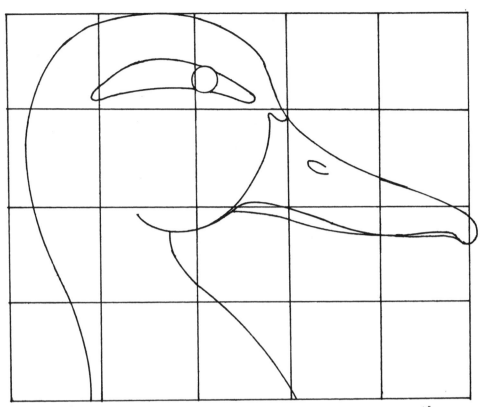

Pintail head pattern.   1″ squares

Widgeon head pattern.   1″ squares

1 " squares

Body pattern for canvasback or redhead.

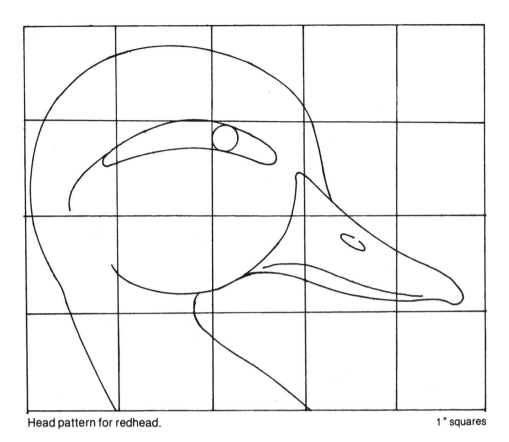

Head pattern for redhead.   1″ squares

even the tightest spots such as under the bill or chin.

The large body-blocks are carved in much the same manner. The old-timers merely used a sharp hatchet to rough shape these blocks, but that was a skill learned from many hours and many wasted blocks. For most of us, a large wood rasp or sculpture's wood chisel works best; or you can utilize one of the metal wood rasps that fits in a portable electric drill. As in any type of carving, take your time and make sure you don't carve or chisel into the grain or you may knock off a large splinter that will ruin the block. Carve completely around the decoy, a little at a time as you go, so it takes shape overall, rather than concentrating on one area right at the first. Final shaping should be done with a wood rasp.

Then use progressively finer grits of sandpaper to finish the blocks to a smooth surface without any chisel or rasp marks. A "flap sander" in a portable electric drill will speed up this chore, but you must keep the sander moving or you'll gouge the surface of the block.

Test fit the head on the top of the body to ensure that the flat part of the head will fit down properly on the body. You may have to do a bit of reshaping to ensure a flat spot for the head to fit down on.

The heads are held in the blocks with dowels through them and into the blocks. Position the head securely in a wood vise and use a nail or centerpunch to mark the exact center of the flat on the bottom. Using a good, clean, sharp ⅜-inch drill bit in a portable

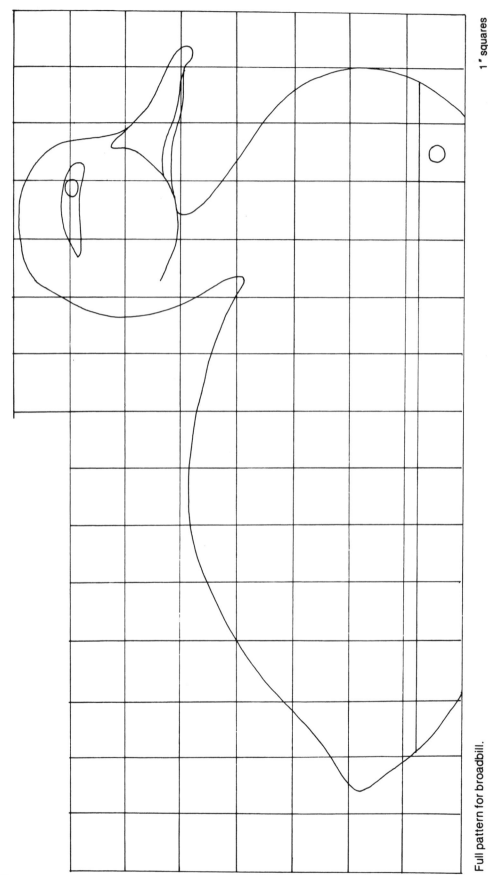

1" squares

Full pattern for broadbill.

Full pattern for (solid blocks) Canada or snow goose.

1" squares

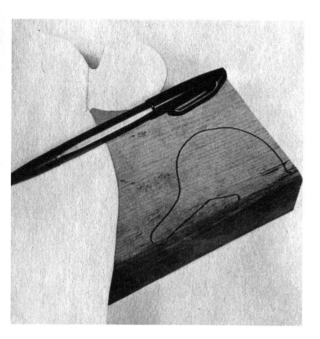

Make a template from heavy cardboard and transfer it to the wood.

Bandsaw out the outline of the head.

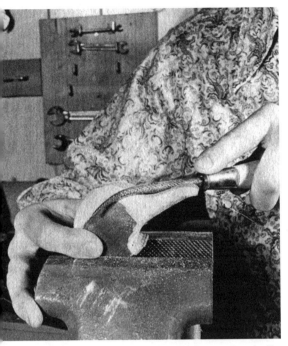

Using small wood rasp, sharp carving knife, etc., carve head to rough shape.

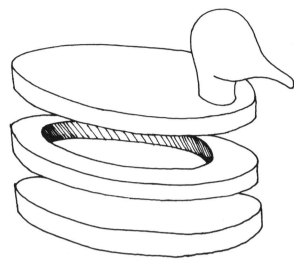

Wood decoys should be hollow to cut down on weight.

Sand body and head as smooth as possible. A "flap sander" in a portable electric drill makes this job fast and easy.

Bore a ⅜-inch hole in neck and insert a wooden dowel.

electric drill or a hand drill, bore a hole in the head for the dowel. Make sure that you keep the drill bit straight up and down, not slanted to one side or the other. To keep from drilling completely through the head, measure about ¾-inch on the drill bit and place a piece of masking tape as a mark or drill stop.

Glue the dowel in the head and position the head, measure about ¾ inch on the drill location of the dowel hole. Again use a centerpunch to mark the location of the dowel and bore with a ⅜-inch bit. Glue the head in place using waterproof glue. The head can sit straight, pointing straight ahead, or turned sideways, whichever you prefer. Mix them up, some decoys with heads turned each way and some pointing straight ahead. That is one of the advantages of making your own decoys. You can get a greater variety in your set of blocks instead of having them all look alike.

Finally, shape and rasp the areas around the neck and body to blend them in properly. You may wish to use a bit of wood putty to smooth and blend the neck and body together. Allow it to dry thoroughly and sand smooth with sandpaper. Allow the head and body to set overnight or until the glue sets, then final sand the decoy using progressively finer grits of sandpaper until the entire decoy is smooth.

Painting the decoy is probably the hardest chore, but unless you're going to be using the decoy as decoration, merely simulate the color patterns, using the simple painting patterns as shown. Decoys can be painted with anything from special formulated decoy paints to exterior latex house paints to acrylic artist colors. One of the advantages of using acrylic paints is that they can be mixed to provide subtle colors to more closely match those in the real waterfowl. The main thing is that the decoy should not shine. The paints must be dull and flat with no chance of a glare to spook

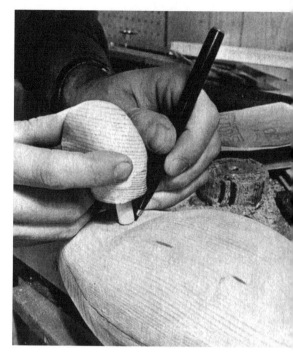

Locate the position of the doweled head on the body and bore a 3/8-inch hole at that location, making sure the hole is bored straight up and down.

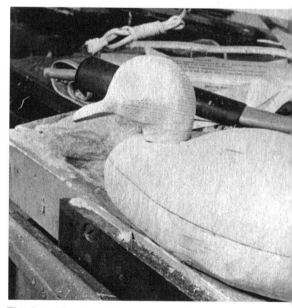

The head is glued to the body with the dowel. Note the head may be turned at an angle, it doesn't have to sit straight with the body.

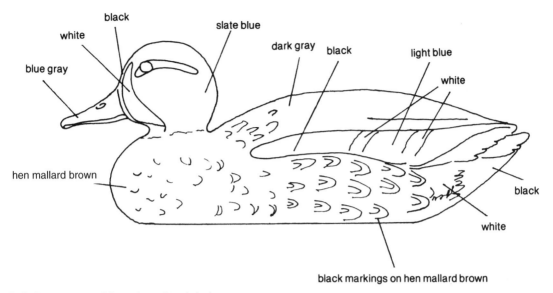

black
white
blue gray
slate blue
dark gray
black
light blue
white
hen mallard brown
black
white
black markings on hen mallard brown

Painting patterns: blue-winged teal drake.

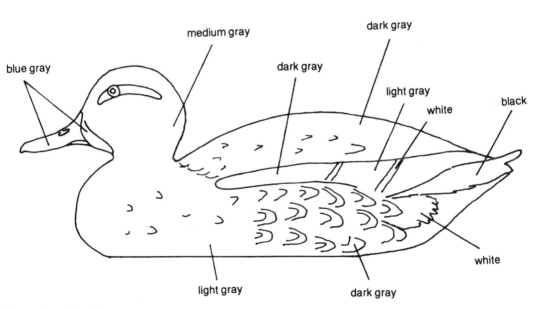

blue gray
medium gray
dark gray
dark gray
light gray
white
black
white
light gray
dark gray

Blue-winged teal hen.

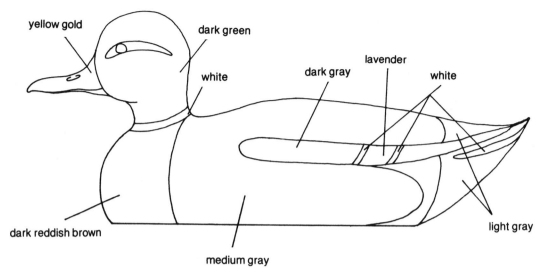

yellow gold

dark green

white

dark gray

lavender

white

dark reddish brown

medium gray

light gray

Mallard drake.

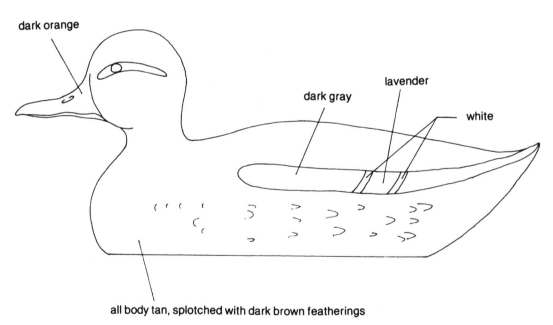

dark orange

dark gray

lavender

white

all body tan, splotched with dark brown featherings

Mallard hen.

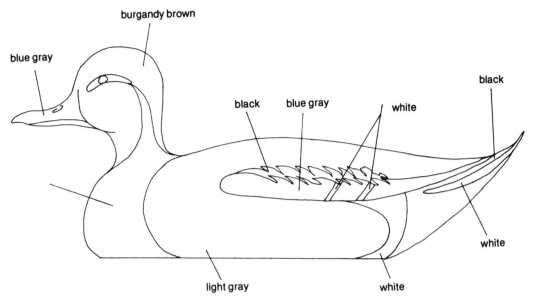

Pintail drake.

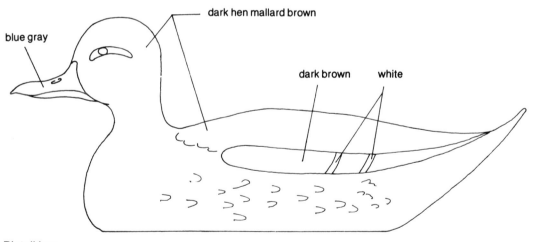

Pintail hen.

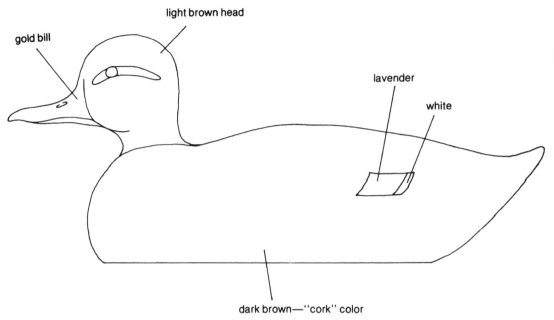

Black duck (both sexes alike).

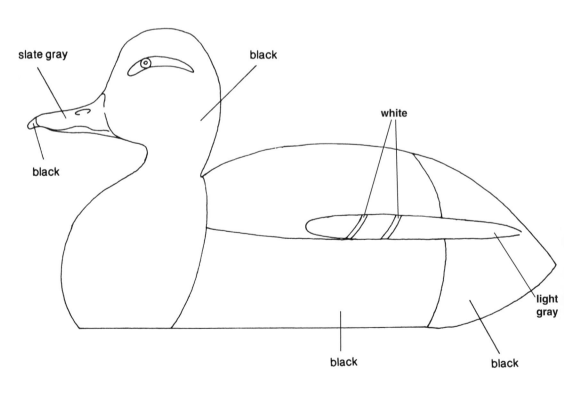

Broadbill drake.

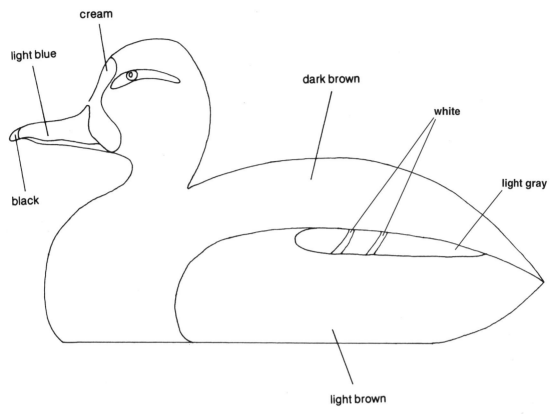

Broadbill hen.

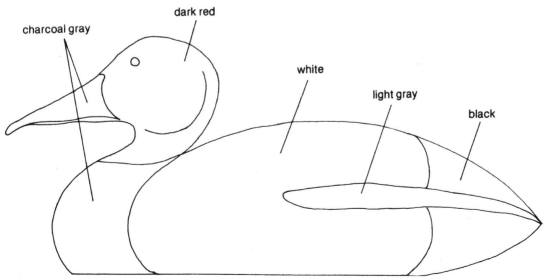

Canvasback drake.

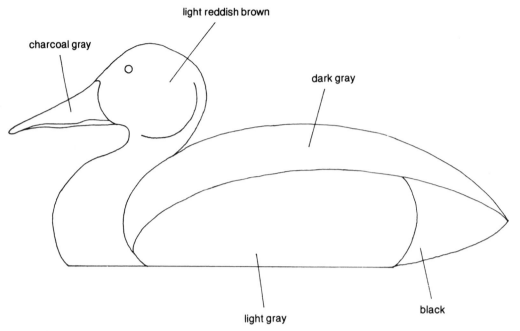

Canvasback hen.

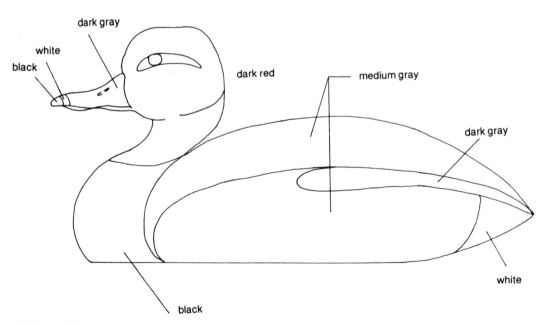

Redhead drake.

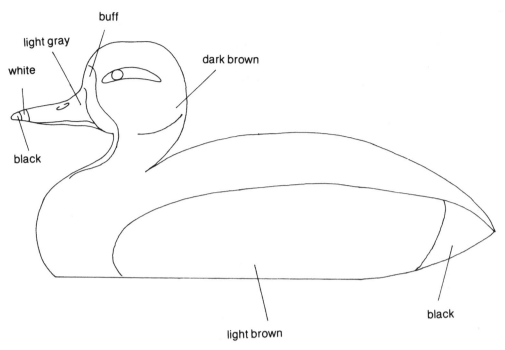

buff

light gray

dark brown

white

black

black

light brown

Redhead hen.

the waterfowl. If you choose to use an oil-based paint, first give the block several coats of a warmed linseed oil. Warm the oil next to a stove or radiator, but watch it carefully to prevent it from getting too hot and starting a fire. It doesn't have to be hot, just room temperature. Make sure you wipe away any excess linseed oil from the surface. If you plan to use exterior latex or acrylic paints, prime the decoy with a coat of exterior latex paint. Regardless of what type of paint you choose, sand the decoy after priming to remove any wood grain that might have been raised.

Paint in the pattern you choose. The feathering is put on by first making a half-moon stroke with a small brush. Allow this to dry somewhat, then dip the brush in paint, stroke off some of the paint, and use the "dry" brush, dragging it across the surface to blend

the moon-shaped strokes and give a stippled look. It's a good idea to paint the lighter colors first, then use the darker colors to paint over any mistakes you might have made. Make sure you get the underside of the chin and bill painted in. The underside of the decoy should also be painted with several coats of paint to protect it.

The eyes can be painted in or you can add more realism by using taxidermy eyes. These are glued in small depressions bored in the head using a ⅜-inch bit with a wide cutting end. Merely bore enough so the eye is somewhat recessed. Do this job carefully, fitting the eye in place a little at a time, then reboring until the eye fits properly. Glue the eye in place with household glue such as used for plastic airplanes, and clean away all excess glue. Touch up the paint around the eye to match the head.

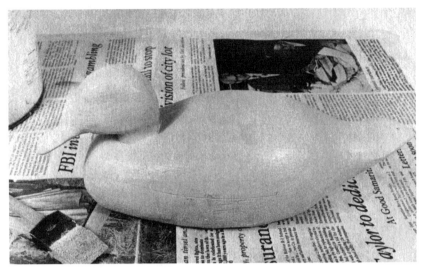

Final sand the entire decoy and give it several coats of a warmed linseed oil, or you may prefer to prime it with a good grade of exterior latex paint.

Paint in the pattern chosen. You can use special formulated decoy paints, exterior latex, or acrylic artists' paints, but any paint used must be flat with no luster or shine.

Glue in the eyes or paint them in. The eyes shown are taxidermy eyes. First bore a small depression for the eye to fit down in.

Finished (wooden) blue-winged teal without center keel and rigging.

Decoys can also utilize cork for the bodies, with wooden heads and bases.

CORK

One way of cutting down on both the weight and the amount of time needed in carving is to use cork for the bodies of the decoys. The heads are still carved from wood, but the bodies are carved from large chunks of cork such as is used in lining walk-in coolers and refrigerators. Although the cork is somewhat crumbly and won't shape as nicely, if you stick to simple shapes the decoy will turn out fine. The cork is first glued to a piece of ¼-inch marine plywood to make a solid bottom. Then the glued-up block is rough-cut on a band saw and shaped with a large wood rasp or by using a disk sander.

Holes are bored in the top for the head and the head doweled in place. This is one method of making the larger decoys such as full-bodied Canada goose decoys. The heads on goose decoys are cut from a 1 × 12 and the dowels glued in the ends of the neck. The holes are bored in the top of the cork body for the head dowel, but the head is not glued in place. During transport the heads can be removed and carried separately. To use the de-

coys, merely stick the dowel in the hole in the top of the body.

After building and painting the decoys, the next step is the rigging. Although a simple screw eye can be used to tie the anchor line to

Head is carved in the same manner, but body is shaped from cork.

Rigging.

the decoy, a better method is to use a 1½ × 1-inch "keel" glued and screwed to the wooden bottom. A hole is bored in the front of the keel to tie the anchor line to. This keel keeps the decoy from rocking excessively in rough water, and also helps the decoy to head into the wind in calm weather.

The line used for rigging should match the color of the water and should be of nylon or some water-resistant material.

ANCHORS

Anchors for decoys can be almost anything from paper cups poured full of cement to special lead anchors. To make the cement cups, gather up several of the small household paper cups. Mix cement and pour in the cups. Before the cement sets up, place a bent-over nail in the top as an anchor tie. Or you can make up your own lead anchors. One simple method is to bend a piece of wire into a loop. Heat lead in a ladle until it melts. Then

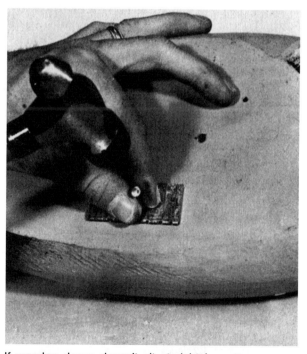

If wooden decoy doesn't sit straight in water, adding a bit of lead weight to one side or end will help.

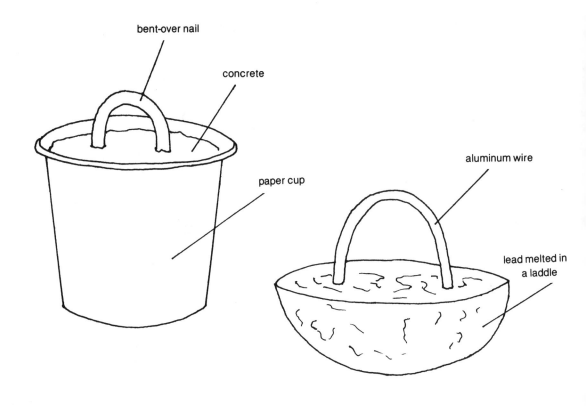

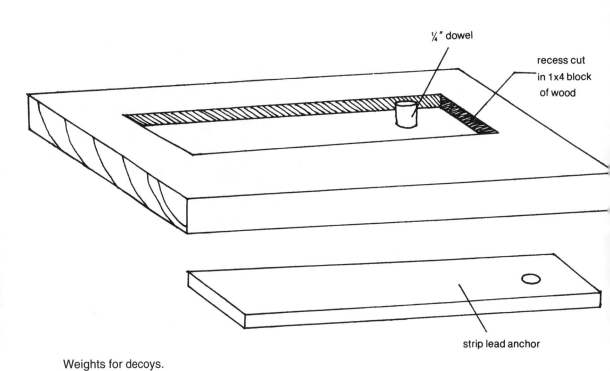

Weights for decoys.

merely stick the wire loop in the melted lead, allow to cool, and pull the completed anchor out of the ladle. The wire loop should be made large enough to fit over the head of the decoy. This makes an easy way to handle decoys with no problems of tangled anchor lines. Or you can rout out a small flat area in a block of wood, glue in a small dowel in one end of the routed area, and pour a "strip anchor" of lead. If using a soft lead, the anchor can be wrapped around the decoy neck during transport.

SILHOUETTE DECOYS

Silhouette decoys, such as used for Canada or snow goose hunting, are the easiest to make. And it's a good thing, because with today's wary waterfowl you'll need lots of decoys. The flat decoys can be cut from ¼-inch marine-grade plywood, then both sides painted. When making several dozen of these decoys, make sure you utilize every bit of plywood that you can from a sheet so there won't be any waste. It's a good idea to make a cardboard template first, and try fitting it on the plywood sheet to determine the

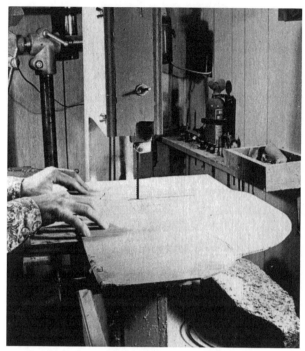

Cut decoy from a ¼-inch sheet of exterior or marine-grade plywood.

best method of cutting. Cut the decoys from the plywood using a saber saw or band saw, and sand the edges using rough sandpaper. Paint the decoys in the pattern desired.

The decoys are held in the ground by wooden stakes screwed to the plywood bodies. Again make some of the decoys with feeder or down-turned heads and some with heads up. It's a good idea to have more feeder heads than alert heads so the geese will not become wary.

DOVE DECOYS

Doves are fast becoming the number-one upland game bird, and as a result more and more hunters are taking to the field after them. Although an area may have an abundance of doves, the birds become extremely wary after a few days of hunting. One trick I have used is to pick a tree with little foliage on

Silhouette decoys are easy to make. Cut from thin sheets of exterior plywood.

1″ squares

Canada goose pattern.

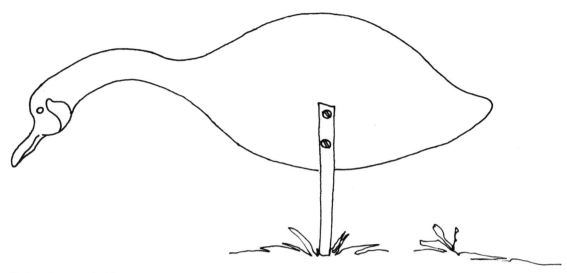

Stakes fastened with screws hold decoys in ground.

Dove pattern.

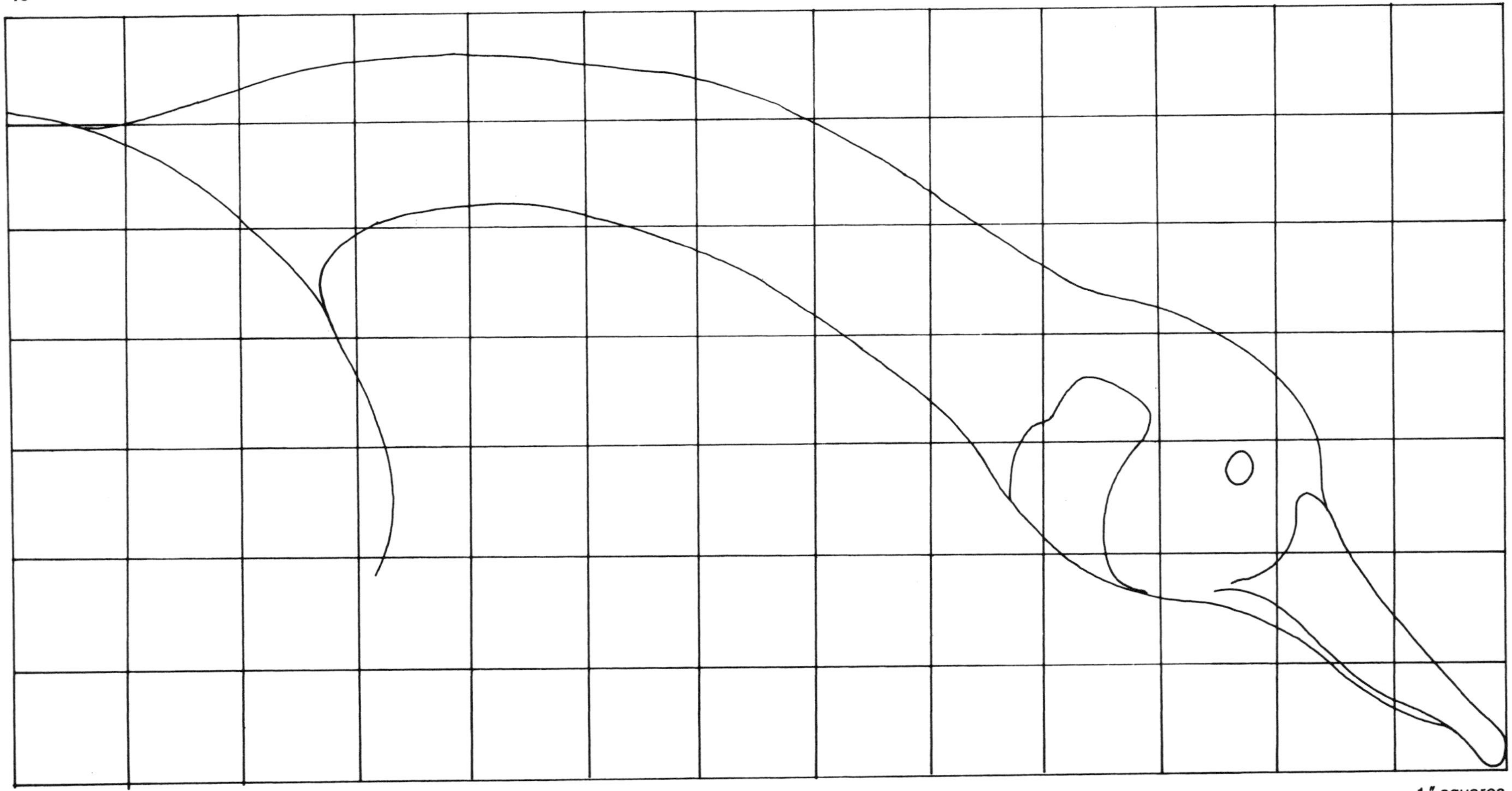

152

1 " squares

Feeding head pattern.

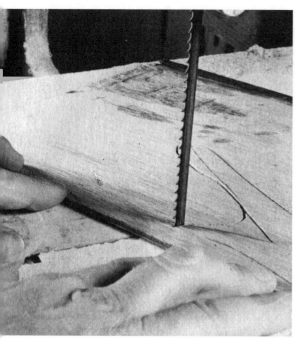

Cut from old sheets of paneling and paint a dull gray.

the boundaries of a grainfield. Normally the doves will fly to such a tree to look over the field before flying into it. The trick is to be concealed and allow one or two doves to alight in the tree. As soon as that happens, doves will start coming in from everywhere. Use the same method using decoys. These are made of scraps of paneling or thin plywood and are merely cut to shape with a saber saw or band saw, then painted a dull gray. The eyes are painted in and wire hooks fastened in the top of the decoys through a small hole. To use the decoys, hang them on thin tree limbs (much like decorating a Christmas tree), find a good hiding spot, and get ready.

Dove decoys are also easy to make and will help a great deal in hunting hard-hunted areas.

9

Bird and Animal Calls

One of the first hunting techniques learned by man was how to imitate bird and animal sounds. Even today in many types of hunting, calling is the most important part. For instance, when duck hunting the big thrill is in talking a flight of ducks down into your decoys, which isn't easy with today's hard-hunted and wary waterfowl. No two people are alike and mass-produced game calls just don't fit everyone. Some people like a loud call, others a soft call; some have thin lips, other heavier lips—and all these contribute to how the call sounds. If your buddy sounds great, but you don't, regardless of how much you practice, maybe your call doesn't fit.

Making your own game calls is quick, easy, and economical. Although most calls are turned on a lathe and are quite fancy, you can actually make the same type of call by merely whittling it out. The Indians made similar calls from saplings that had been allowed to dry and cure for a month or two. Game calls are the most personal items an outdoorsman can own, and they make great gifts for your buddies. I have had several handmade calls given to me as gifts and they are among some of my most beautiful and cherished items.

DUCK CALLS

Some Indian hunters were quite proficient at calling ducks and geese by mouth, but they also had a duck call that was two pieces of hollowed out sapling. A piece of birch bark was placed between the two pieces, and they were laced tightly together. Today's goose and duck calls are made on much the same line.

There are two basic types of duck calls, the marsh or Cajun and the Glodo or Arkansas call. The main difference between them is in the size of the hole in the keg. The hole in Cajun calls is quite a bit larger than those in Arkansas calls. The larger holes produce a loud call that is more effective in the open Louisiana country. The Arkansas call, on the other hand, is made for the potholes and flooded timber, and the smaller hole provides a more subtle tone. The Cajun calls are harder to learn how to use. The Arkansas calls are the ones normally sold over the counter in most sporting-goods stores.

The outside shape of the call can be made in an infinite number of patterns. The keg and barrel are made in two separate pieces and pushed together.

A duck (or goose call) is nothing more than a musical instrument, almost a combination trumpet and clarinet, and everything you do in building it will determine the tone. Calls can be made of almost any even-grained, stable wood. They are normally made of hardwood, not only because it carves better and lasts longer, but because the tight grain makes a better sounding call. I have calls made of red cedar, Osage orange, zebrawood, and many different kinds of walnut—and every call sounds different, just as each and every call from a dealer's shelf will sound somewhat different. That's the fun of making your own calls; you never know just how the

A typical duck call.

sound is going to come out until the call is finished. But since it takes very little time and material to build a call, you can experiment all you wish.

The wood you use must be well cured. "Green" wood will shrink, crack, and probably lose tone entirely. The reed for the call is cut from a 4 $\times$ 5 sheet of photographic film.

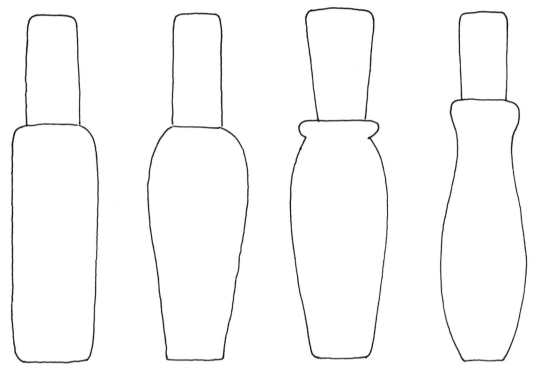

Patterns for outside of calls.

This is available at photo developing stores and portrait shops, or you can purchase reed material from call manufacturers.

The first step after selecting the wood for the call blank is to choose a pattern that suits you. Make a template from a piece of cardboard. Although the call can be hand carved, it is much easier to make by turning on a lathe. Place a piece of stock in the lathe and turn the barrel of the call. Occasionally stop the lathe and check the turning with the template to ensure that you get it turned properly. Leave the turned barrel attached to the waste stock on both ends and make sure one end is square.

Sand the barrel while it is still in the lathe, removing all chisel marks and bringing it down to a fine satin-smooth surface. Note the decorative rings cut in the barrel; although these aren't necessary, they do provide a bit of

personal identification. Cut the top waste portion off the barrel, but leave the square waste section on the bottom.

Stand the barrel upright on a smooth flat surface and clamp it solidly with a pair of wooden screw clamps or a drill press vise. Make sure the barrel blank is standing straight up, not leaning to one side, and that it is down flat on the table. Then bore the hole through the barrel. The hole should be located first and started directly in the center of the top of the barrel with a small drill or awl. Then using a ⅝-inch forstner or flat-bottom bit, bore entirely through the barrel making sure the bit goes into the waste stock. Set the barrel aside at this point.

Turn the keg. Many call makers like to turn the keg of a contrasting type or color of wood from the barrel to make a more attractive and unusual call. Use a pair of calipers to make

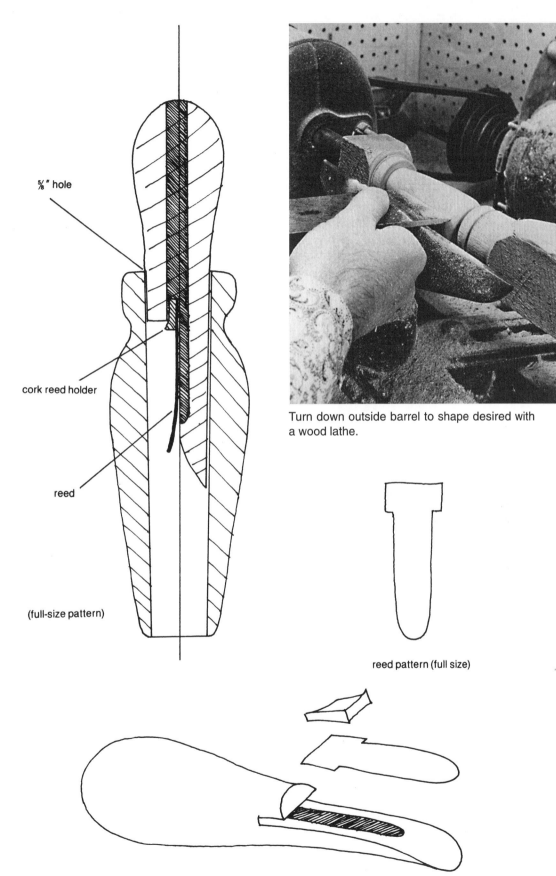

⅝″ hole

cork reed holder

reed

(full-size pattern)

Turn down outside barrel to shape desired with a wood lathe.

reed pattern (full size)

Inside duck call pattern.

Leave the bottom of the barrel waste on the blank. It should also be left in the square stage and the bottom end should be square with the blank. Cut off the top of the blank.

Place barrel blank in a wood clamp or other drill-press vise, making sure it is positioned straight up and down and bore a hole entirely through it with a ⅝-inch bit.

Remove keg turning from lathe and cut off ends. Then place keg in barrel and bore the sound chamber hole to the proper depth and size. Some calls such as goose calls also have a recessed larger hole in the upper end. These should be bored first so you can locate them in the center of the call. Then bore the deeper hole with the smaller bit.

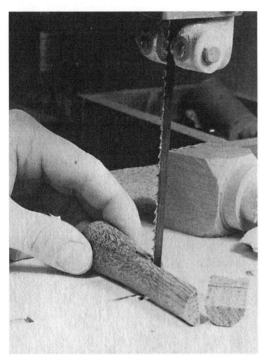

Remove the keg and cut it to shape.

sure the keg will fit in the barrel hole properly. When you get the proper shape and size, sand thoroughly while still on the lathe.

Remove from the lathe and cut off the waste from the keg turning. Insert it in the barrel. When the keg fits in the barrel properly, place it in position in the barrel and bore a ¼-inch hole in the keg. Again, the easiest method of boring is to use a drill press. Lock the barrel upright securely in a base or wooden clamp, place the keg in the barrel and center punch for the correct position of the hole, then bore.

Remove the keg, cut off the waste from the barrel, and shape and sand it smooth. Cut the proper shape on the end of the keg for the tone chamber and reed holder. Sand and smooth it thoroughly.

Cut the reed from a piece of 4 × 5 or 8 × 10 developed film. You may have to cut and experiment to get just the right shape and size

of reed for the tone you want, so cut several blanks. Place the blank in position over the tone chamber in the keg and cut a small piece of leather or cork to wedge the reed in place. Unlike many older types of calls, your new call can quickly and easily be taken apart for repairs or to clean it out.

With the reed and reed holder in place, fit the keg into the barrel and try the call. If the call is too high pitched, you will need a new reed blank because the reed is too short. If the call is too low, cut a tiny bit, not more than ¹⁄₁₆ inch, off the end of the reed. Don't shift the reed in the call to achieve a good tone; the reed will eventually lose its place and it will take some time to get it properly located to retune the call. Instead make sure the reed fits the call properly and snugly and produces the right tone. Then cut several other reeds in similar size and shape.

When the call is working properly, remove the reed and reed holder and finish the call. This can be done by dipping the individual pieces in an acrylic or marine varnish, or by spraying with a high-quality outdoor finish such as a gunstock finish. The pieces can be finished separately or together. After the finish has dried, smooth with steel wool.

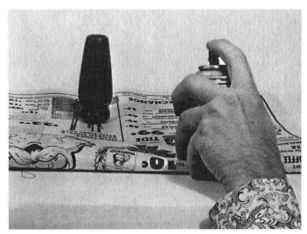

Install reed, tune call, and spray finish with a good gunstock finish.

GOOSE CALLS

Goose calls are made in the same manner as duck calls, except the outside shape is normally changed a bit so the waterfowler can wear both calls or carry them in his pocket and be able to quickly and easily identify the one he needs by merely grasping it.

The basic difference between goose calls and duck calls is that the reed in the goose call

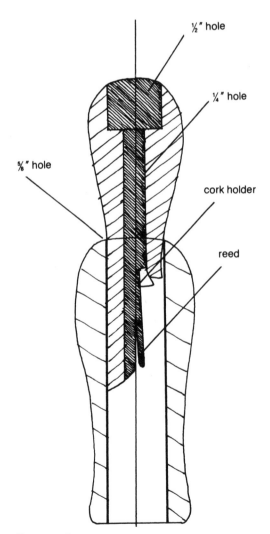

Goose call.

is normally cut somewhat smaller but the entrance hole in the keg (not the tone chamber hole) is cut quite a bit larger.

Construct the goose call in the same manner as the duck call.

If you wish, you can make a different type of goose call. It is constructed much like a cedar box turkey call and is based on a Seminole Indian pattern. A box is made from a ¹⁄₁₆-inch piece of cedar, sanded smooth, and glued together as shown. A thin flat stick is shaped like a paddle and a piece of shale or slate is glued to it. In use, rosin is rubbed on both the slate and the top edges of the box. Then the slate is drawn back across the edges of the box. If drawn slow and easy, the sound will be the low guttural sound; if the sound paddle is jerked and pushed down a bit harder, the high pitched sound will emerge. It takes practice, but with patience you should be able to imitate an old honker pretty well with this simple little call.

CROW CALLS

Calling crows is both challenging and fun, and you can quickly and easily make your own crow call. You will need two short sections of dowel; use a 1-inch or closet-pole dowel and a ⅝-inch piece. Cut the two pieces to length and clamp them in a wooden clamp, then mark the barrel and bore it completely through with a ⅝-inch bit. Make sure it is standing straight up and is not leaning to one side or the other. Place the keg in the wood clamp and bore it with a ⅜-inch bit so about ⅜ of an inch is left. Round off the closed end, then saw the keg in half. File down the inside flat portion of the ends just a bit and cut a reed of photo film to fit between the two sections. Push the combination reed and keg pieces into the barrel and experiment with the sound. By filing more off the lips or rounded end of the keg, you can change the sound. When the sound

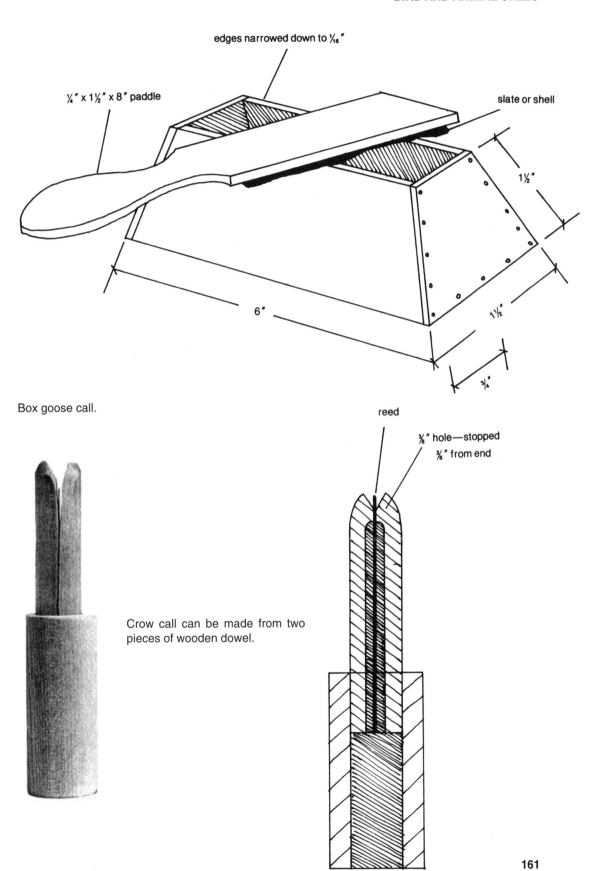

edges narrowed down to ⅟₁₆″

¼″ x 1½″ x 8″ paddle

slate or shell

1½″

6″

1½″

¾″

Box goose call.

Crow call can be made from two pieces of wooden dowel.

reed

⅜″ hole—stopped
⅜″ from end

Clamp the larger piece of dowel in a wood clamp and bore it through entirely. Then bore the smaller dowel only to depth shown in the drawing.

Round the end of the reed holders and shape them slightly concave on sandpaper.

Cut reed material from film and install between holders, fit in place and try call. When it wc properly, glue holders and reed in barrel of call.

is right, glue the two keg pieces into the barrel and wipe with several coats of lightweight finishing oil, making sure you don't get any down in the barrel or reed and sound chamber.

VARMINT CALLS

Making a varmint call is as easy and as much fun as using it. You can make a turned call exactly like the crow call. The only difference is in shortening the reed and narrowing it down a bit to get the high moaning sound.

A much simpler method is to cut a couple of 6-inch pieces from a wooden yardstick. Using a rasp or pocketknife, cut a 2-inch-wide notch in one side of each piece. Place a large rubber band (about ¼- to ½-inch wide) over one piece end to end and then tape the two pieces together. Blowing across the rubber band produces the sound. By cupping your hands in different ways, or moving the rubber band between the wood strips (pulling it tighter), you can create different sounds.

Varmint call. This varmint call is one of the easiest calls to make. Cut two 6-inch lengths of a yardstick. File a depression across the yardstick pieces in the center.

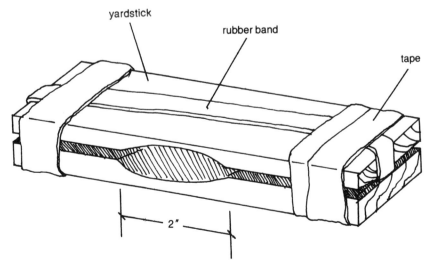

Varmint call.

One of the best turkey calls can be made from a block of cedar wood.

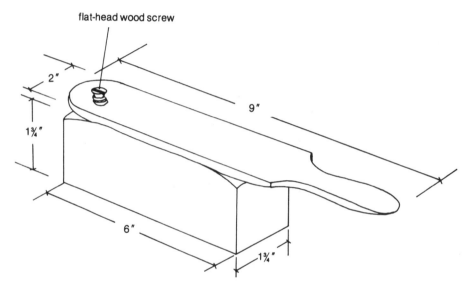

flat-head wood screw

2"

1¾"

9"

6"

1¾"

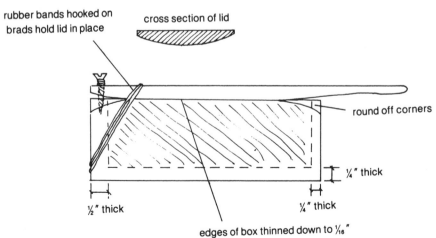

rubber bands hooked on brads hold lid in place

cross section of lid

round off corners

¼" thick

½" thick

¼" thick

edges of box thinned down to ⅟₁₆"

TURKEY CALLS

Hunting and calling wild turkeys is one of the most challenging of outdoor sports. Almost everything has been used to make calls to fool the wily old tom turkey; however, time has narrowed the field down to several tried and true types of calls.

BOX CALLS

The easiest call for beginners to make and to learn to use is a box call, traditionally made of cedar. It can be made in two different ways: by gluing thin cedar pieces to make up a box, or by carving a hollow box out of a solid chunk of cedar. Purists say the solid block makes a better, more resonant-sounding call. To make the solid-block call cut the block to the proper size, then place the block on a drill press and mark the outline of the box opening. Bore holes to the depth of the inside of the box with a forstner bit, then use a sharp chisel to remove the waste wood left from boring the holes. When the box is rough shaped, use a fine chisel to smooth up the inside. Surface the top and side edges of the box. They should be thinned down to about ⅛ inch and sanded perfectly smooth.

Make the handle-lid section of the box (note that it is thicker in the middle than on either edge). Round this portion with a wood rasp, then sand it smooth. Fasten the lid to the box with a single screw from the end opposite the handle. The lid must swing and work freely on the pivoting screw. A small spring between the lid and the screw head will help position the lid properly. Traditionally these boxes aren't finished because any finish might deter from the sound. But they should be well smoothed and sanded throughout. A rubber band can be used around the box to hold the lid in place when not in use.

To hollow out center of box mark outside outlines, then remove material with a series of bored holes. Use chisel between holes to remove the rest of the waste.

Rub a piece of chalk over the edges of the inside surface of the lid, then gently scrape it back and forth across the box side to get the yelping sound of a hen turkey. The thickness of the edges will determine the pitch. You might wish to make one edge thinner than the other so you can produce both a gobbler and a hen sound. By turning the box upside down and shaking it, you can produce a gobble.

WINGBONE CALLS

These calls date back to the Indian days. Although they're easy to make (if you have the

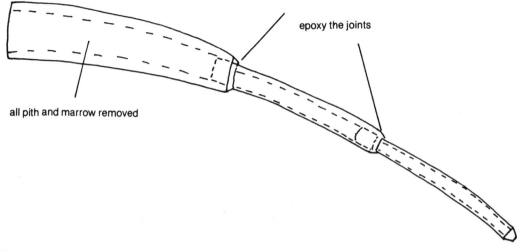

epoxy the joints

all pith and marrow removed

Wingbone.

wing bones of a turkey), they're somewhat hard to learn how to use.

Cut the bones from the wing where the joint is at the body. You won't need the wing-tip bone. Clean the bones carefully, then cut off the ends to expose the pith. Clean out all the inside marrow with a fine wire. Place the bones in boiling water to re-move the inside entirely, then glue the end of the small bone into the larger bone with epoxy cement. The joint must be completely airtight.

In using the call, place the tip of the call in your mouth, just slightly off center, then suck in as in kissing. It takes a bit of practice to make the call work.

10

Blinds

ALL-PURPOSE PORTABLE BLINDS

One of the simplest yet most effective blinds I have ever used is made of camouflage netting and lightweight wooden stakes. These blinds can be made in any size. I have hunted out of one large enough to hide a boat in, as well as one barely large enough for one person to crouch down in.

Use sharpened wooden tomato stakes for the blind support pieces. Staple a piece of deadgrass or regular pattern camouflage netting to the stakes, which should be spaced about 2 to 3 feet apart. It will take six stakes for a small one-man blind, and about a dozen for one large enough to hide a boat in. The blind can be carried quickly and easily into the field and set up. If the hunting isn't particularly good where you're located, you simply pick up the blind and move it to another area. When hunting in water, smear some mud over the cloth to help blend it in with the surrounding area. If using the blind in the backwoods for deer or turkey hunting, cut a few small branches and place them around the blind. If you leave the blind up,

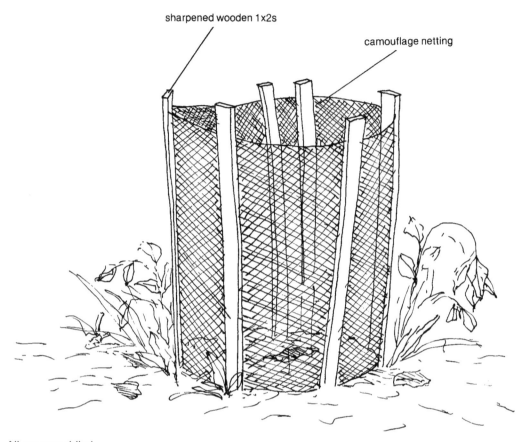

sharpened wooden 1x2s

camouflage netting

All-purpose blind.

the branches must be fresh each day; the appearance of dead leaves may make the game a bit wary.

I also like to keep several pieces of different colored camouflage netting in my pickup. I can always hunker down or even lie down and throw one of the nets over me for a fast "make-do" blind. This has made many a day, for instance when I notice a flock of geese working a field while driving somewhere. After getting permission to hunt, I drag out a camo-net blind and head for the field.

DUCK AND GOOSE BLINDS

I have shot out of everything from a fancy enclosed blind complete with telephone service back to the main lodge, to a rusty, old, cold, steel barrel sunk in a riverbank. Blinds

for waterfowl have literally been made from almost everything imaginable. The most effective blinds, regardless of what type they are, are those that blend in with the surrounding area. For instance, a wooden blind thatched with reeds would look totally out of place on a rocky coast.

PALLET BLINDS

One of the most economical blinds I ever shot out of was made entirely from wooden pallets. Using pallets or skids 38 × 50 inches, you can make a blind that will comfortably seat three hunters. The pallets are rectangular in shape and two are placed on their sides for the front of the blind. Two are stood on end for the back, with the space between them being used for the doorway. A pallet cut on an

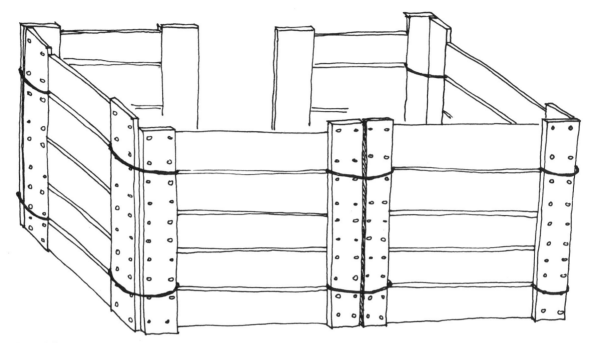

Pallet blind.

Blind is held together with plumber's strap.

angle is used for each end. A 1 × 12 "roof" can be added to provide more concealment; old wooden boxes are used for seats. The pallets are held in place with plumbers strap nailed to them as well as good old-fashioned baling wire. Paint them a dull brown color, then float them across the water on a boat to the spot where you wish to build the blind. Assemble on the spot and camouflage with tree limbs and marsh grass well before hunting season starts. When the season ends, it will be an easy matter to take down the blind and remove it.

CONCRETE SUNKEN WATER BLINDS

One of the most effective, longest-lasting blind is a sunken water blind made of concrete. These are also expensive—and naturally they're permanent. For year-to-year

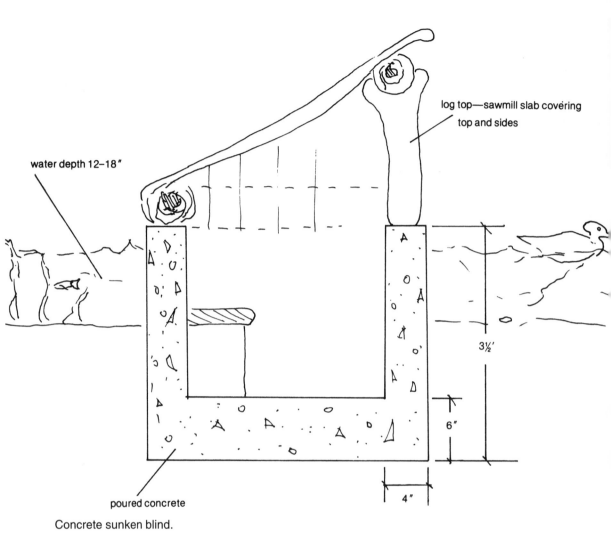

log top—sawmill slab covering top and sides

water depth 12–18″

3½′

6″

4″

poured concrete

Concrete sunken blind.

gunning of an area that consistently proves out, they just can't be beat for comfort.

They are also normally used in ponds or marshes where the water level can be controlled. They are built using plywood forms poured with concrete. The top of the front opening of the blind should be from 4 to 6 inches above normal water level of the surrounding area. Sometimes these are located in river bottoms and each year they must be cleaned of mud and debris from the spring flooding times. The top portion of the blind may be metal, concrete, or wood de-

pending on the choice of available materials. I have shot out of a sunken concrete blind with a log top for many years. It is situated deep in a timbered bottom pothole and blends in perfectly. The blind is sunk in the ground and is surrounded with about 18 inches of water—ideal for mallards and pintails.

Building this type of blind is quite a job, especially if all materials, including the concrete, have to be transported to the site. The concrete should be reinforced thoroughly and a good watertight mix should be used. You can coat the inside of the blind with basement waterproofing paint and coat the outside with black asphalt to help cut down on leaks.

BANK BLINDS

A variation of the sunken water blind is the "bank blind." It is normally used on small potholes or ponds and is sunk in the back side of a dam or levee bank. The front opening edge is placed almost level with the ground, and the back door can be walked into from ground level. (It's sort of a "split-level" blind.) These can be made of concrete or metal. I have also seen this type of blind made out of logs, although the logs would eventually rot.

WOODEN PIANO BOX BLINDS

The most popular type of blind is probably the wooden "piano box" blind, which may be

placed on levees or even on platforms or stilts above the water. They're made of wood and can often be constructed at home, then hauled to the site. A friend of mine who operates a duck hunting club builds them on giant runners. He then pulls them to where he needs them and moves them around as the hunting season changes.

They can be constructed from marine plywood or rough-sawn sawmill lumber depending on your choice and the availability of materials. Naturally the plywood blinds will be tighter, but they will also be quite a bit more expensive. The plywood must be painted a dull color while the rough-sawn wood will eventually fade to a dull gray. It will, however, warp and twist a great deal.

Staples or sections of woven wire should be fastened to the outside of the blind to tie on camouflaging materials.

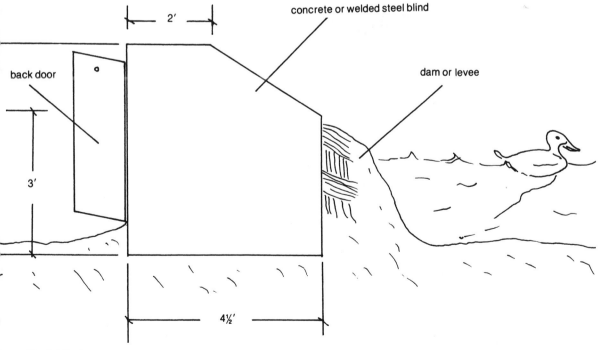

Bank blind.

Uncamouflaged wooden piano box blind on pilings in water.

Camouflaged piano box blind.

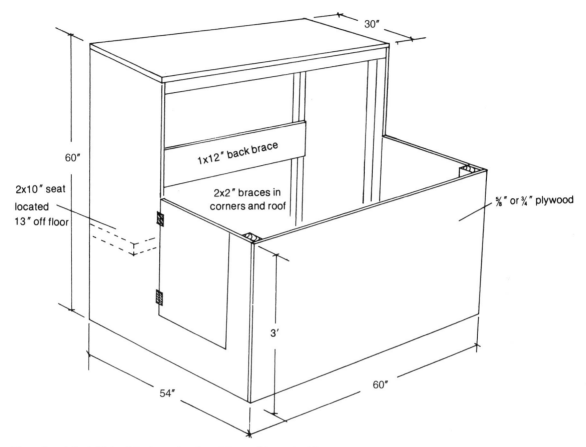

Piano box blind. Note: blind can be 4 or 5 feet wide on inside.

GOOSE PITS

There is nothing colder than a goose pit. They are just what they sound like—pits dug into the ground, normally in a milo or cornfield. They can be anything from a simple hole dug in the ground and lined with plastic sheeting to an elaborate concrete or metal blind sunken entirely in the ground. The latter is naturally expensive and takes a great deal of time to build. It also must be located in a good flight pattern to ensure the return of the investment. The blind can be made of concrete poured from forms, or it can be made of metal. One metal goose pit I have shot out of was constructed of a large discarded gas barrel with the top cut out.

The top of the blind was fitted with a hinged frame of chicken wire with camouflaging material attached. You could see out, but the geese couldn't see in; and when they were within shooting distance, it was simply a matter of flinging back the top to get into shooting position.

After digging and installing the blinds, all material removed from the excavations should be carried away from the field.

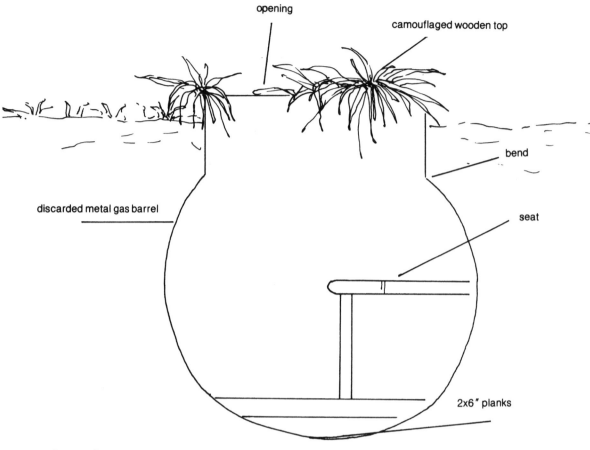

Goose pit.

BARREL OR COFFIN BLINDS

These are small barrels or wooden boxes sunken in the ground near a good shooting flight path. They are normally lined with marsh hay for warmth, and a light covering of camouflage is placed on top of them. They are extremely effective blinds for those areas where the amount of work in installing them would be worth it. They should be installed well before the season, and all excavation material should be removed from the site.

PHOTO BLINDS

Probably the most effective blind is your automobile. I have shot some of my best wildlife photos while slowly driving along country lanes. Animals are not particularly afraid of automobiles and will let you get quite close, but shut off the motor or try to get out and they will vanish in a hurry.

Another effective blind is a small tent. It can be pitched in a good spot and the camera set up. Bait the area with grain or corn for birds and small animals, or with dead meat for such animals as coyotes.

LADDER BLINDS

One of the most frequently photographed subjects is a bird on her nest. To enable you to get better closeups, build a small lightweight photo blind on a step ladder. The step ladder and blind can be set up and then left for a

lined with marsh hay

Barrel or coffin blind.

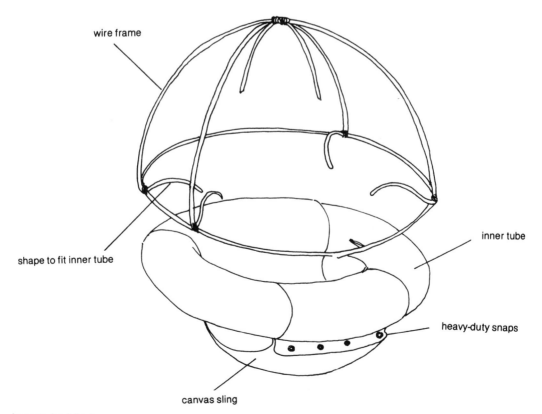

wire frame

shape to fit inner tube

inner tube

heavy-duty snaps

canvas sling

Inner tube blind.

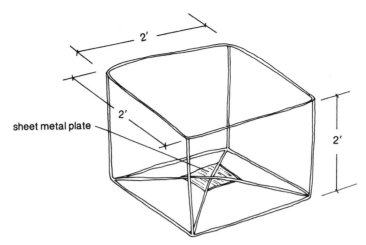

sheet metal plate

2'

2'

2'

Ladder blind.

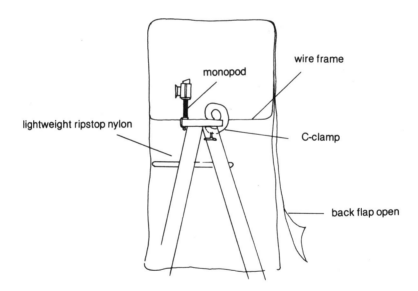

monopod

wire frame

lightweight ripstop nylon

C-clamp

back flap open

time. The blind should not be used until after the bird has become used to it. The step ladder should be sturdy and the blind well built; the bird or animal will become alarmed if the blind moves or shakes.

An effective blind for photographing ducks and other water birds can be made from an old inner tube covered with camouflaging so it looks like a muskrat nest. Blow up a truck inner tube and measure it for size. Make a canvas sling seat to fit. The camouflaging is supported by heavy-duty wire formed into a dome.

The wire dome is first covered with camouflage netting, then dead grasses, etc. Used with chest waders and floating the "blind," you can slowly sneak up very close to waterfowl.

11

Tents and Shelters

Making your own tents may seem a bit challenging, but you'll find it is a great way of extending your outdoor fun into those cold, winter do-nothing months. In addition, you can make high-quality articles at an economical price.

TENT TYPES

Tents come in a variety of sizes, shapes, and styles and making your own is fairly easy if you stick to the simple, basic shapes. Knowing something about sewing will help, although it isn't absolutely necessary. The old-timers made their tents out of heavy-duty canvas that had to be waterproofed every year and weighed a ton. Today you can choose from lightweight, fireproof, and water-resistant cotton duck or drill, or lightweight ripstop nylon. The nylon is available in both nonwaterproof and urethane-coated waterproof material. In fact, the nylon material is so waterproof that if a tent were made of it entirely it would be thoroughly wet very shortly from condensation forming on the inside. As a result, most

Regardless of whether your camping is backpacking or horse-pack hunting, you can make your own tent.

nylon tents are made with urethane-coated nylon bottoms only. The rest of the tent is made of uncoated ripstop nylon. A rain fly made of either urethane-coated or non-coated ripstop nylon is placed over the tent to protect it from rain.

If the canvas material is used to make a tent, you will probably have to sew it on a heavy-duty machine, although I have had friends who were able to sew the canvas on their home sewing machines. When sewing a bottom in a tent, you will be sewing through at least four layers of material. Experiment to see if your particular machine will handle the heavy-duty material. On the other hand, if using the lightweight nylon to make the tent, an ordinary home sewing machine can be used. Both nylon and canvas material are available in widths up to 45 inches.

First step is to make a pattern, then transfer it to the material you're using.

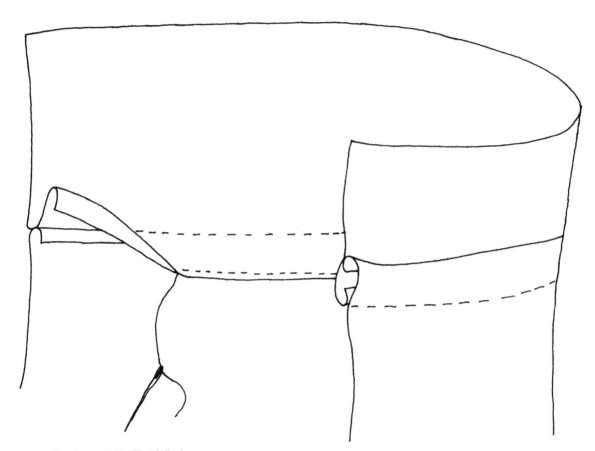

Sewing details. Flat-felled seam.

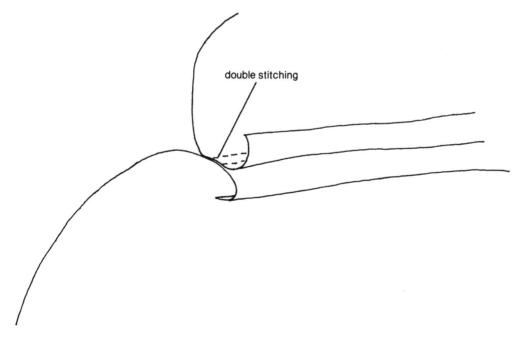

double stitching

Double-stitched seam.

The basic tent is cut out and sewn in the same manner as in sewing garments. The thread used is a cotton-wrapped Dacron thread.

When joining the panels of a side or back together, use the flat-felled seam, as shown. Note that the seam is sewn, then one side is trimmed to ¼ inch to cut down on bulk, then the top overlapping portions are sewn down into a neat "tube." This seam leaves no raw edges on the inside or outside of the finished tent. For added strength this seam can be top stitched once or twice more in addition to the one line of top stitching required to make the seam. The seams where different sides of the tent meet are sewn in a simple double-stitched seam with the tent turned wrong side out. Don't forget to place the guy rope tabs, or pole support tabs, in place during the sewing. All unfinished edges (such as on rain flys and the front edges of tents) should be turned under at least twice and then sewn into a hem.

Tent Poles

In the old days when a camper wished to put up a tent, he merely cut some saplings for support poles or tied a main support rope be-tween two trees. With today's restricted camp-sites and crowds of campers, that is no longer possible. You can, however, purchase "replacement poles," or you can make your own tent poles using ¾-inch do-it-yourself aluminum tubing sold at most hardware stores. The ends of the poles are made to fit in the tent grommets by shouldering a 3-inch length of wood dowel. Sand or rasp the dowel so it will fit snugly in the end of the tubing, then bore a small hole through the tubing and dowel and drive a flathead nail through. The nail must protrude completely through the tubing. Cut it off so about ⅛ of an inch sticks through the tubing, then peen this over to make a rivet to hold the wooden end in place.

Extension poles are made in the same manner. The wooden dowel is shaped to fit in both poles. The dowel is fastened in one end of one of the poles using a nail as a rivet.

Grommets

All tie loops or other places where tent poles support the tent should be reinforced with grommets through the tent material. These metal rings are easily installed on the tent material using a grommet-setting kit, available at leading sporting-goods stores.

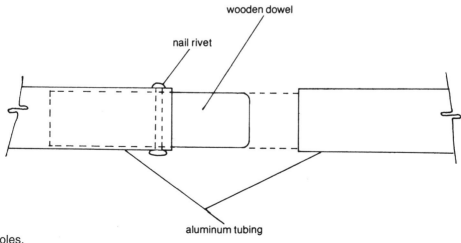

wooden dowel

nail rivet

aluminum tubing

Tent poles.

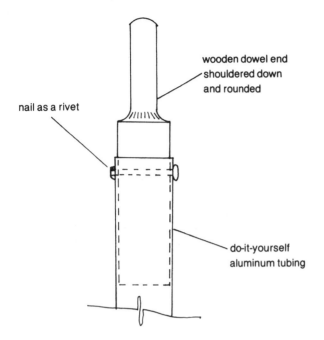

wooden dowel end
shouldered down
and rounded

nail as a rivet

do-it-yourself
aluminum tubing

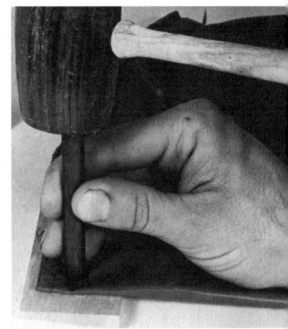

Grommets for guy ropes or tent poles are installed using a grommet setting tool. First step is to punch hole in material.

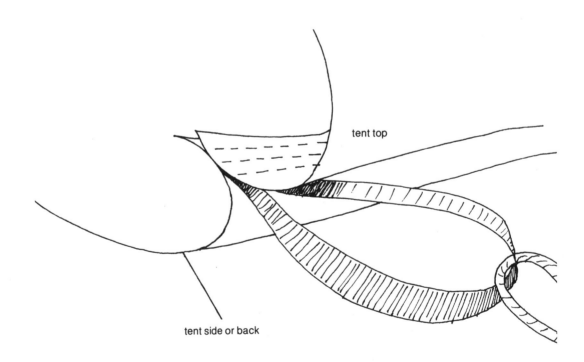

tent top

tent side or back

Adding tie tabs.

Place bottom of grommet in anvil.

Then place material over grommet bottom and place top grommet ring in place.

Use special grommet setting punch to tap the grommet pieces together.

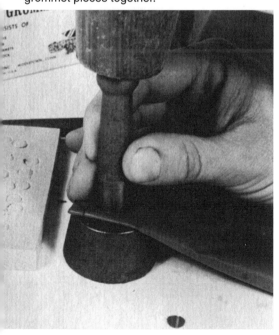

The finished grommet . . . quick and easy.

Tent Pegs

To make heavy-duty pegs for larger tents, cut a ⅜-inch reinforcing rod into 1-foot lengths with a hacksaw. Bend the loop on the top to tie to. Although these pegs are heavy and cumbersome, they're great for automobile camping and will hold heavy-duty tents secure.

Lightweight pegs for backpacking tents can be made from ¼-inch hardwood. Saw to shape on a band saw and sand smooth. Make sure the line notch is filed and sanded smooth so it won't cut through the tent guy lines.

Tent Fly

Although waterproof nylon can be used to make tents, it won't breathe or allow air and moisture to escape from the tent. As a result the tent becomes covered on the inside with condensation. The solution is to make the tent from ordinary nylon material and make a fly or covering piece of material from water-proof nylon. In good weather, the fly can be left off entirely; in bad weather, it can be placed over the tent. The fly and tent should be constructed so that there is some air space between them. Make the fly in the same manner as the tent, doubling the seamed edges for strength and placing grommets in the areas needed.

PONCHO TENT

One of the simplest tents you can make is a combination poncho/survival tent. Made of lightweight urethane-coated nylon, it can be used both as a rain poncho and as an emergency tent as well. The first step is to make an 8 × 8-foot-square piece of fabric. Double the outside edge and sew a seam around it. Place grommets in each corner and one in the middle of both the front and back. Make a hood from the pattern shown of the same material. Sew a drawstring seam around the front edge of the hood. Cut a hole in the center of the

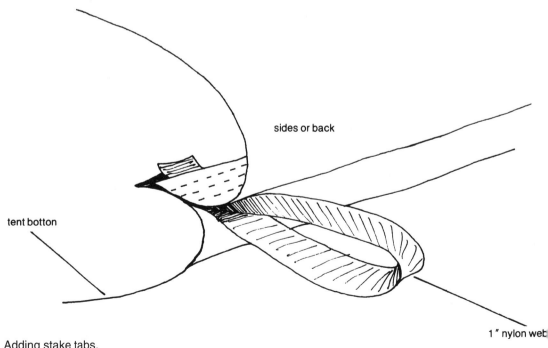

sides or back

tent botton

1″ nylon web

Adding stake tabs.

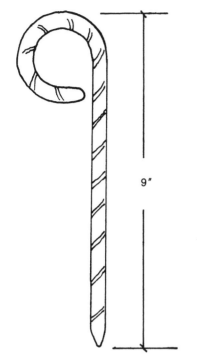

9"

metal and concrete reinforcing rod pegs

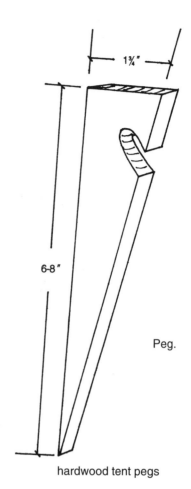

1¾"

6-8"

Peg.

hardwood tent pegs

fabric piece for your head to fit through and sew the hood in place over the hole. Place a piece of nylon string through the hood as a drawstring. Waterproof all seams with tent seam waterproofing material.

The tent can be used as a protective covering in an emergency or pitched as shown. If you wish to make it even more effective as emergency equipment, paint the underside in a reflective color.

BAKER TENT

If you don't like the closed-in feeling some tents give, you might consider the baker tent, an old-time design that is one of the most efficient for backcountry camping. In cold weather, the front is hinged and can be swung up out of the way so a fire made with backlogs can be built in front of the tent. The en-tire tent acts like a giant reflector. It's also a great tent for watching the stars overhead or the flames from a flickering campfire. You can tie the front to stakes overhead as a rain fly. During the day the front can be dropped to cover the opening.

The best size for a baker tent would be 7 × 9 feet—just about right for two people plus their gear. You can make these tents up to 8 × 10 feet in size, although when they're that large they become rather awkward and cumbersome.

Because the baker tent is pitched with a fire fairly close, it should be made of a waterproof, fire-resistant material—lightweight nylon tenting material or 7-ounce cotton

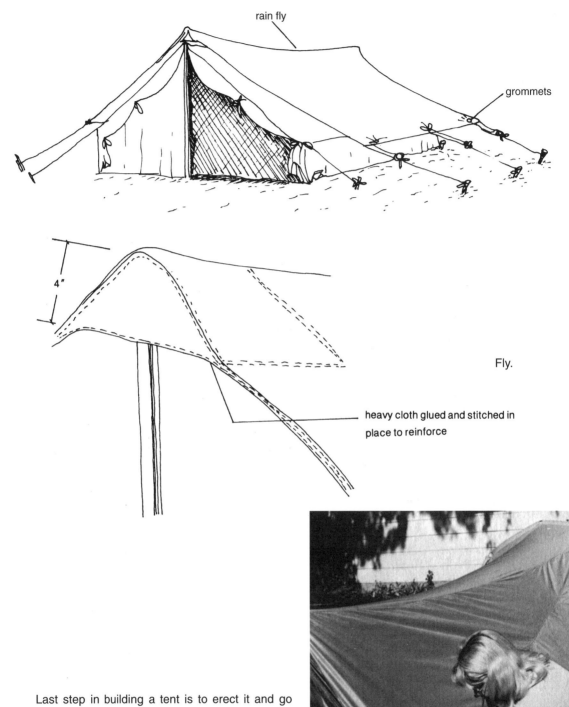

rain fly

grommets

4"

Fly.

heavy cloth glued and stitched in place to reinforce

Last step in building a tent is to erect it and go over the seams with a tent-seam waterproofing material.

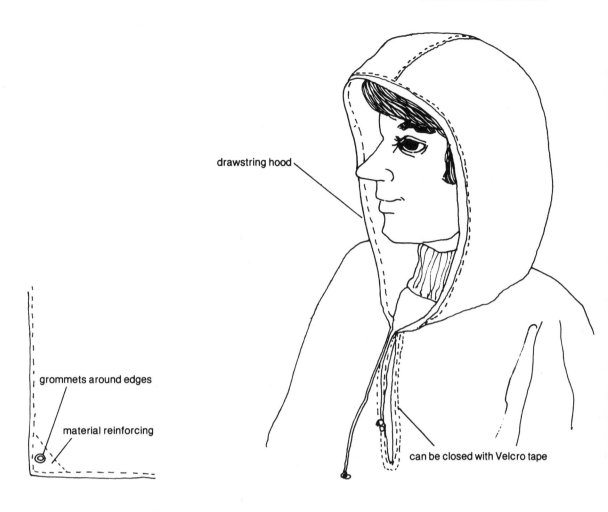

drawstring hood

grommets around edges

material reinforcing

can be closed with Velcro tape

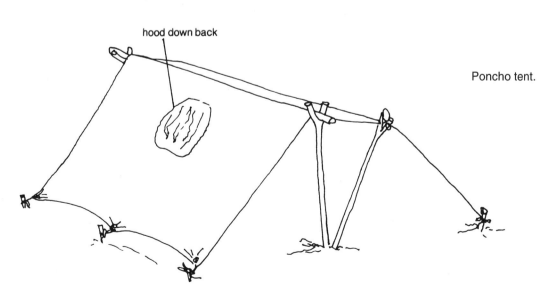

hood down back

Poncho tent.

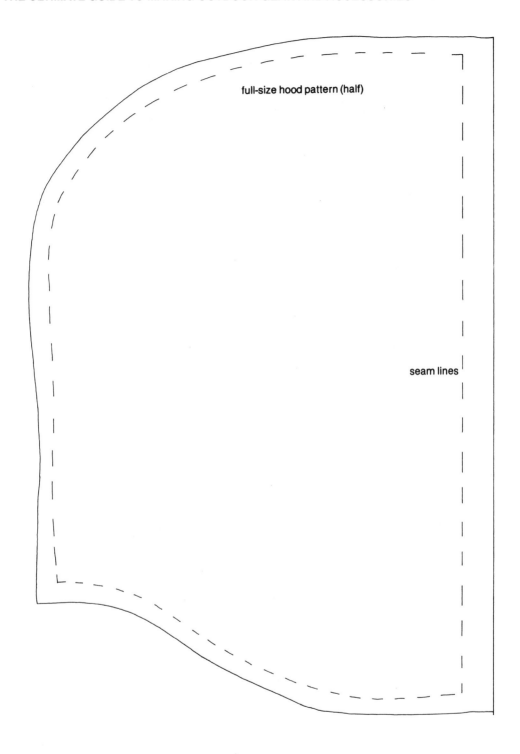

full-size hood pattern (half)

seam lines

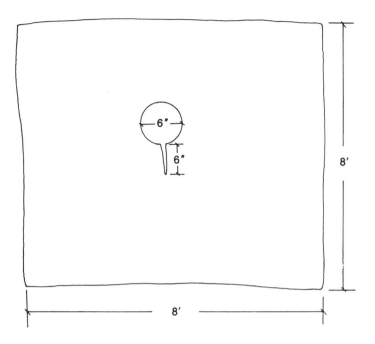

Poncho pattern.

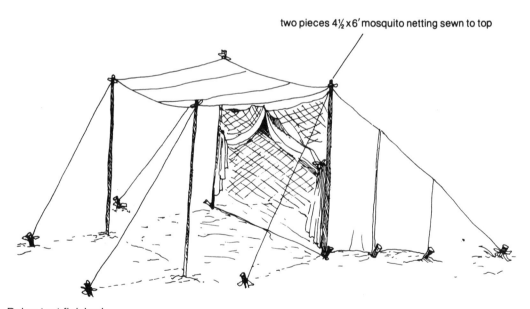

two pieces 4½ x 6′ mosquito netting sewn to top

Baker tent finished.

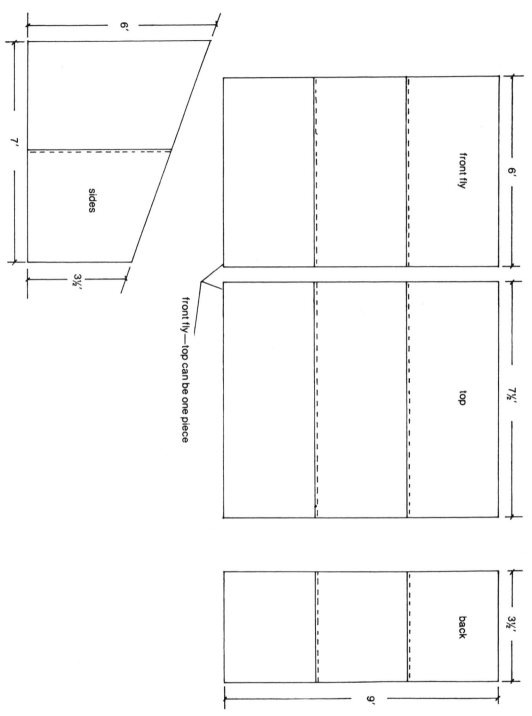

Baker tent pattern.

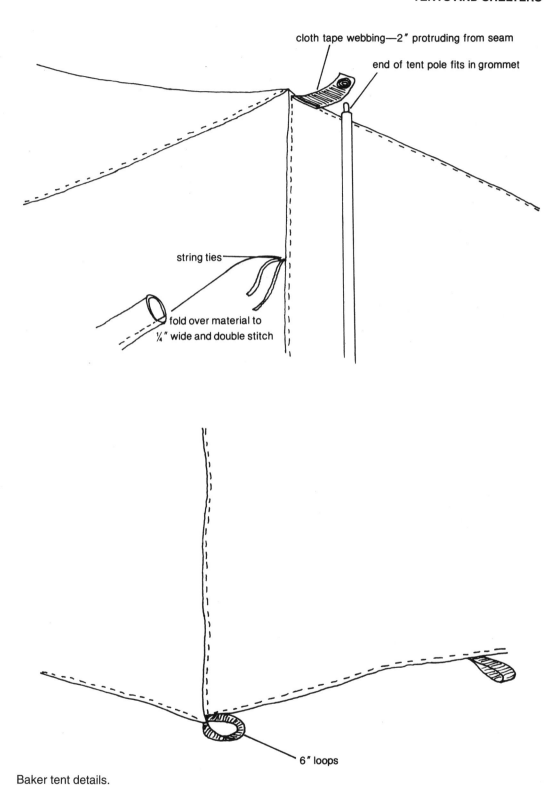

Baker tent details.

duck canvas. The canvas would eliminate the need for a rain fly, which would be a nuisance anyway with this type of tent. On the other hand, you would need a heavy-duty sewing machine to sew the canvas material. The old-timers would have laughed at a baker tent with a screened-in opening and a floor, but it's a good bet although it does make the sewing more of a problem. The choice is yours.

Cut a pattern for the tent pieces from heavy-duty wrapping paper, taping the various pieces together to make up the patterns. Trace the patterns off onto the material and cut the pieces to the right shape and size. Just like in garment making, the pattern should be pinned to the material before you attempt to cut it.

The next step is to sew the two side pieces together using a flat-felled seam. Sew the three pieces together for the back, the pieces for the top, and those for the front as well. If the tent won't have a bottom, fold over the bottom edges of the sides and back and sew a bottom hem. If the tent will have a bottom, leave the pieces at this time.

Sew the back and top pieces together. Note: The three guy rope tabs, made of webbing tape, on the back seam must be sewn in at the same time. Then sew the sides to the back and top. All these seams should be sewn with the tent wrong side out. Hem around the three outside edges of the front fly piece leaving enough space for grommets in the two front corners. Sew the front fly to the front edge of the top of the tent with the tent turned wrong side out. If the front will have a mosquito netting, it should be sewn in at this time. It is sewn to the top only, not down the sides. The two end tabs that hold the poles should be sewn in place. If you don't wish to put a bottom in the tent, sew the stake tabs to the tent. If you are going to use a bottom, place it in, and sew the tabs in place at the same time you do the bottom, with the tent wrong side out.

Although the front and mosquito netting can be secured to the sides by tie strings, a better method is to use Velcro down each side, especially for the mosquito netting.

After sewing the tent, make up the poles, stakes, and guy ropes to the correct size and erect the tent in your backyard. Then apply waterproofing to the canvas material. If nylon was used, waterproof all seams.

MOUNTAIN TENT

Based on a combination pup and wall tent, this small tent is ideal for canoeing, camping, and backpacking. It is made of lightweight nylon with a rainproof fly. It can be made to sleep two to four depending on the size. For two, make it 5 × 7 feet. For four, make it 7 × 9. The smaller tent will weigh between 3 and 4 pounds, the larger about 7 pounds.

The mountain tent is somewhat harder to build than the baker because of the window in the back. There are also more seams and more pieces to cut out and match. The basic tent is made much like the baker tent.

Sew the side bottom panels together first, followed by the top. Then make up the back panel, sewing the mosquito netting window as well as the top edge of the window flap. Follow this by sewing the Velcro on the inside to hold the flap in place.

Sew the sides and top piece together, with the tent turned wrong side out. Remember to sew the three guy rope tabs between the pieces. Sew the back to the sides and top placing the tape for the back poles in between at the tent back. Sew the Velcro to both the mosquito netting doors and the outside doors. Sew the front door half to the sides and top. Remember to sew each door half of both outside nylon and inside mosquito netting, as well as holding tapes for door when opened at the same time. The top for holding the pole must be sewn at the same time.

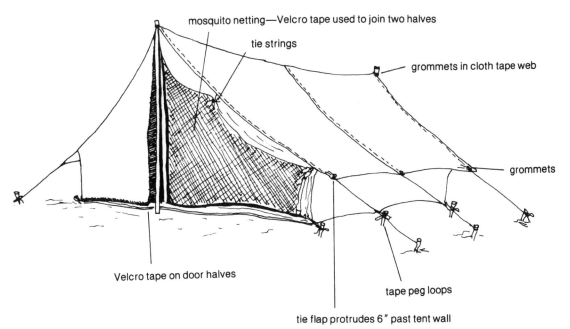

mosquito netting—Velcro tape used to join two halves

tie strings

grommets in cloth tape web

grommets

Velcro tape on door halves

tape peg loops

tie flap protrudes 6″ past tent wall

Mountain tent finished.

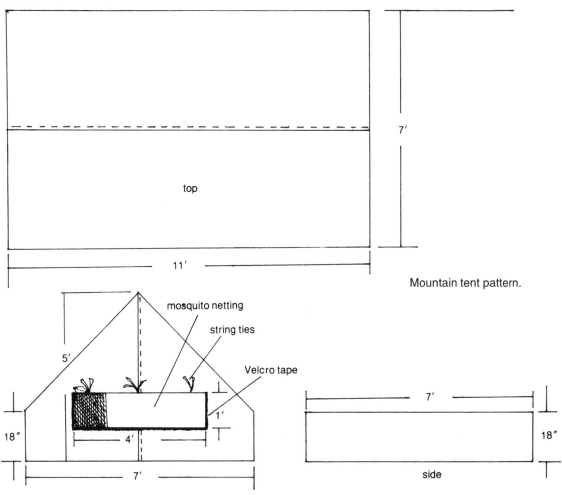

7′

top

11′

Mountain tent pattern.

mosquito netting

string ties

Velcro tape

5′

1′

18″

4′

7′

back

7′

18″

side

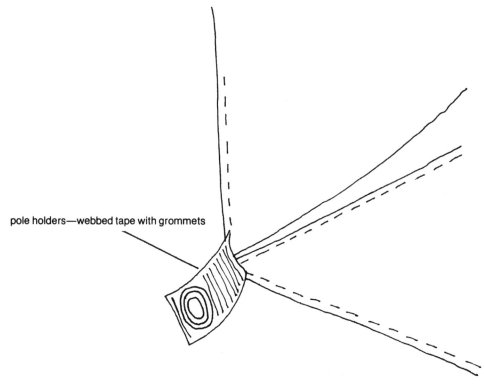

pole holders—webbed tape with grommets

Mountain tent details.

Turn the front floor seam under and hem it. Then sew together the floor pieces of urethane-coated nylon flooring. Sew the floor to the back and sides of the tent while the tent is turned wrong side out. The tabs for the tent stakes must be sewn in place at the same time. Sew the grommets in the tabs, make up the poles and guy wires, and pitch the tent. Waterproof the seams with tent seam sealer.

Make up the fly, as shown, from urethane-coated nylon.

Wall Tent Canvas Materials List:
Sides; 3½ x 11½', 2 reqd.
Top; 11½ x 23', 1 reqd.
Ends; 8 x 11½' x 2 reqd.
Rain fly, waterproof canvas or use a waterproof tarp; 12 x 24', 1 reqd.

WALL TENT

Wall tents are extremely popular for big game and western hunts. They can actually be extremely effective for any camping situation where several campers or hunters must be accommodated. Most wall tents are designed to utilize a stove inside either for warmth while sleeping or as a cook tent. Wall tents can be of just about any size you desire, but the bigger the heavier, and the harder it is to erect. For three to four persons, consider a 12 × 12 foot tent. Actually it's best to have more than one tent, as this provides more privacy as well as a separate cooking tent.

You can make up your own wall tent, and construction is fairly easy, but the most common material is cotton duck, and you will need some means of sewing the heavy canvas. A plain single-roof tent will not, however, shed water. A plastic tarp rain fly is invaluable.

Wall tents are extremely popular for semi-permanent camps.

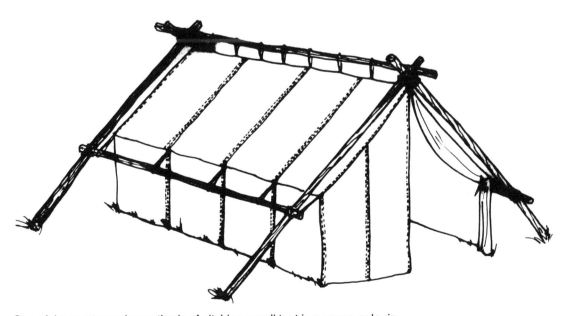

One of the most popular methods of pitching a wall tent is a seven-pole rig.

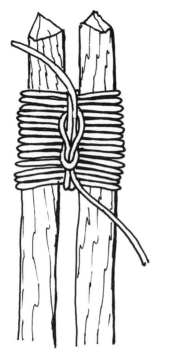

Wall tents are normally pitched using poles cut on the spot, although many wilderness areas require you to pack in the poles as well. Wall tents can be pitched several ways, with the seven pole version extremely popular and sturdy. The front and rear poles are lashed together on the ground side-by-side, then lifted. The lashing tightens as the poles are pushed apart.

First step is to determine the size of the tent. Large wall tents are created from rows of canvas duct. Make up a diagram to determine the size of the various pieces. Then cut and sew the canvas to the correct shapes for each piece. Finally join the pieces to create the tent. You will also have to sew in loops for the rope guys where appropriate, as well as loops for attaching to the top pole. Note: The opening for the stove pipe must be reinforced with fireproof material such as an asbestos or metal pipe guard. The latter are sometimes available at army surplus stores. A sod cloth attached around the bottom can be a great aid in keeping out moisture and wind.

The shear poles are lashed side-by-side ending with a square knot. Spreading the poles apart tightens the lashing.

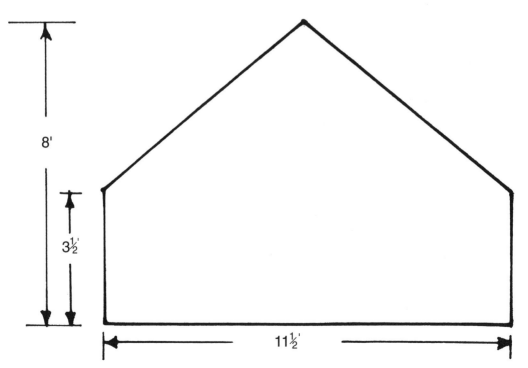

A 12 x 12 foot wall tent utilizing 36-inch wide canvas actually ends up 11½ by 11½ feet.

12

Backpacks, Frames, and Rucksacks

My first attempt at making a backpack was as a youngster. I sewed some loops on an old feed sack and tied the top with binder twine. Although I definitely wasn't ready for the wilderness, this simple rucksack sufficed for my ramblings around the Ozark countryside. Today's backpacks are ultra sophisticated and a far cry from "feedsack rucksacks." You can make your own backpacks and rucksacks for a great deal less than purchasing the manufactured equipment. For instance, a good backpack can be made for about $10, quite a savings from even the economical $35 models. The frames for the pack are made from aluminum tubing while the cloth can be lightweight cotton duck or urethane-coated (ripstop) nylon. Just as in making your own tents or sleeping bags, some basic sewing know-how will help.

FANNY PACKS

These are the simplest packs and are great for day hikes when you want to carry a lunch, binoculars, a sweater or lightweight jacket,

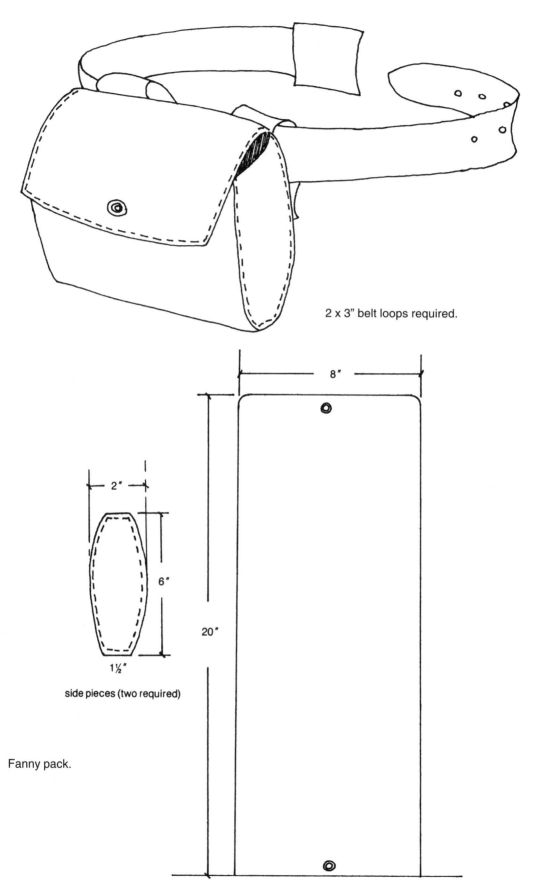

2 x 3" belt loops required.

8"

20"

2"

6"

1½"

side pieces (two required)

Fanny pack.

compass, matches, or other emergency items. I use the fanny pack for deer hunting. The pack is basically just a small pouch that is fastened to a good-fitting leather belt.

Make the pattern and pin it to the fabric, then cut the fabric. The pack is sewn together inside out with an ordinary home sewing machine. The top flap can be held in place with string ties or with snaps. The snaps are placed in the cloth using a special snap-installation tool found at most sewing notion counters.

RUCKSACKS

Rucksacks are a somewhat larger pack carried on your back; actually nothing more than a large sack with a drawstring top. They, too, are ideal for one-day journeys, although they aren't of much use for carrying enough camping supplies for longer periods. The rucksack is made of canvas or ripstop nylon. Again follow the pattern shown to cut the pieces, then sew the pack together. The flap on top is brought down over and tied to close. Pockets can be sewn on the pack if desired. The straps are made by folding the material over three times and sewing the length several times.

BACKPACK CHILD CARRIERS

This carrier is one of the more unusual camping items, and I made mine long before they became popular in camping stores. The frame of the pack is made of aluminum tubing and is designed to be built two ways. The top portion of it stays the same no matter which design you choose, giving junior a handlebar for those rough spots in the road. You can make the lower portion like the carrier shown, enabling you to use the bottom platform as a pack for such items as Thermos bottles and lunches, or you can eliminate the

2″ cloth web or strap material fastened in top middle of back

Rucksack.

bottom platform completely for a somewhat lighter frame.

Bending the frame is easy, but you'll have to have a conduit bender. If you don't own one, or can't borrow one, they can be rented for a nominal cost at the same store selling the conduit. The only thing to remember in bending the tubing is not to make any of the bends any sharper than those shown in the drawing, or you'll probably end up with a kink or two in the curve. This doesn't hurt the performance of the carrier at all unless the metal fractures and causes a rough edge—but it doesn't look as well.

After bending the frame to the shape shown, cut off the protruding long piece

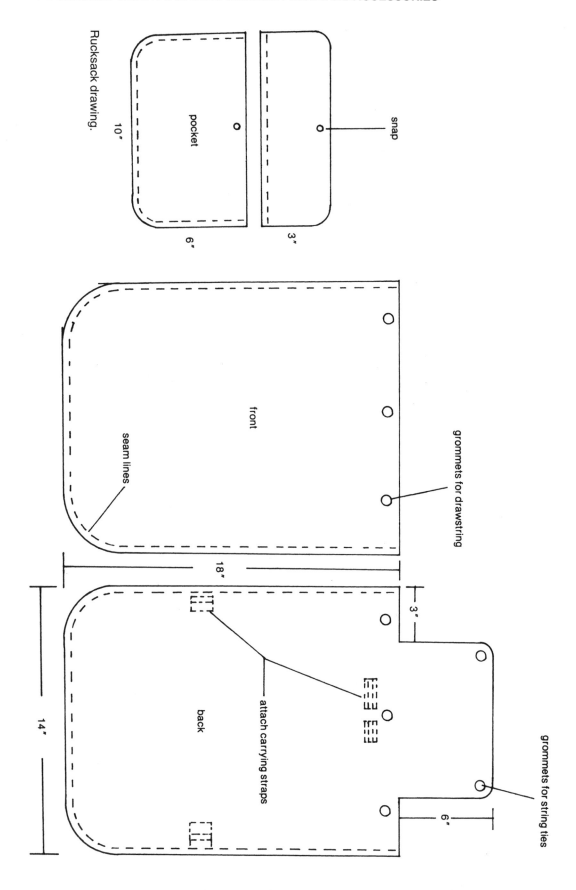

Rucksack drawing.

Backpack child carrier.

pattern on the material with the back of the carrier on the salvage. Cut around pattern. Cut a 5-inch strip from the full length of the material for the strap. This should be at least 60 inches in length and be folded over three times to make a 1- to 1¼-inch strap. Pad covers are cut from the remaining scraps. With right sides of material together, stitch around entire piece except the back. Turn entire piece right side out by pulling through opening left in the back, then top stitch this opening. Bring points A together and stitch down to point B easing curved area. Stitch the other side in the same manner. Place the carrier on the frame and mark for snaps and buttonholes. Attach snaps approximately 1 inch apart to the four sections of the seat that fold over the frame. Make two buttonholes approximately 1½ inches long through the center back fold-over to allow the strap to pass through. From 1-inch-thick foam rubber, cut two pads 1 inch wide and 6 inches long, cover with material, and make a buttonhole on each end for the strap to slide through. Cut a pad 2 inches wide and 12 inches long, cover and snap it around the lower back brace. Adjust straps to proper length and snap or buckle in place. Pack a lunch and head for the zoo or your favorite campsite.

BACKPACKS AND FRAMES

Building your own backpack and frame is a bit more challenging. Like the child carrier, the frame is made of aluminum. The pack is made from mediumweight cotton duck or ripstop nylon. Make the frame first.

Although the frame could be made of hickory saplings, the best choice is aluminum tubing. The tubing requires more work, but it is much lighter and produces a stable, lasting frame. Cut two pieces of tubing to 32 inches. Carefully file down the cut ends to remove any burrs that might have been formed.

and cut the three cross braces from it. Using a ball peen hammer, peen the ends flat and round them over a heavy round pipe to fit the rounded contour of the tubing. Position them in place, drill holes through both the cross braces and frame and pop rivet in place. File off all rough edges and sand the entire assembly satin smooth with steel wool.

Making the Seat and Straps

The cloth portion of the carrier requires about 2 yards of 39-inch material. Any heavy material, such as cotton duck, will do. Although the material is heavy, you should still use a double thickness for the carrier. Fold the material lengthwise and lay the enlarged

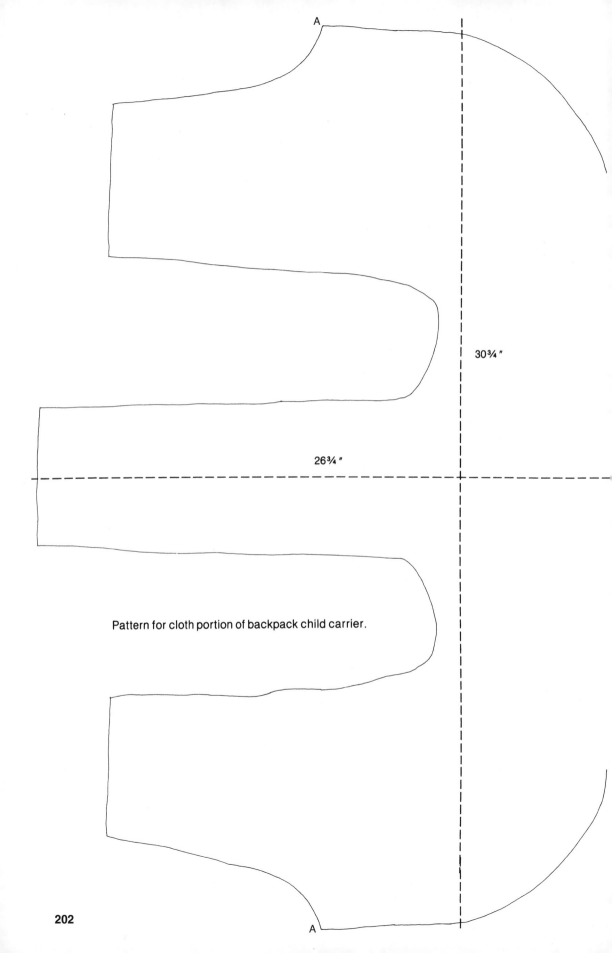

A

30¾ "

26¾ "

Pattern for cloth portion of backpack child carrier.

A

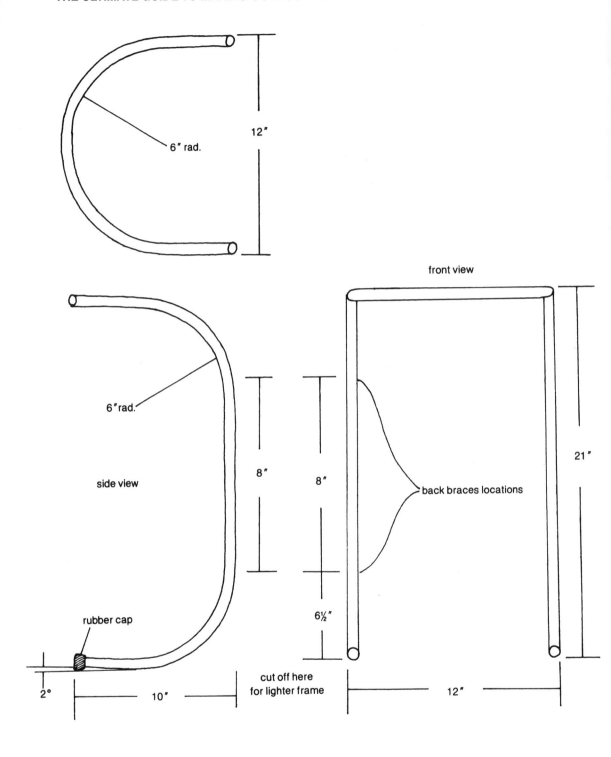

12″

6″ rad.

front view

6″ rad.

side view

8″

8″

back braces locations

21″

rubber cap

6½″

2°

10″

cut off here
for lighter frame

12″

Child pack frame.

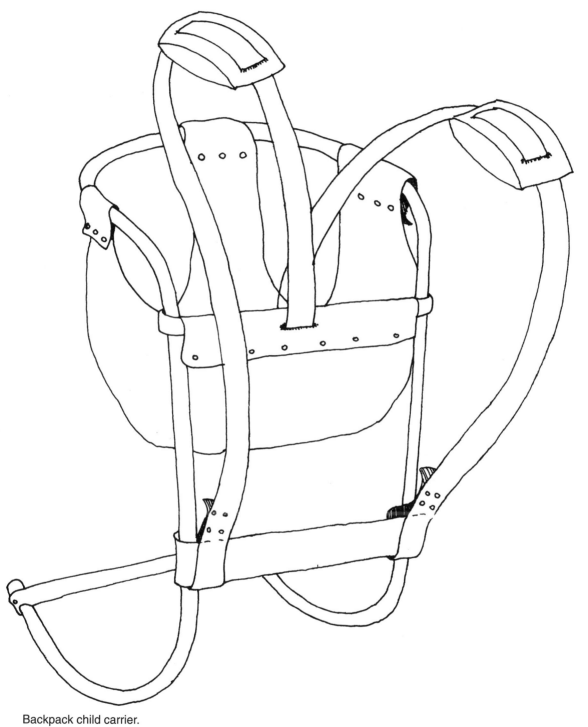

Backpack child carrier.

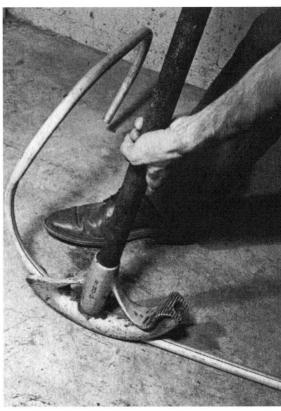

Lightweight aluminum tubing is easily bent with rented or borrowed conduit bender. Measure for second bend and carefully shape pipe.

Third bend goes in an L. To keep from kinking bends, radius of bend should not be less than 6 inches.

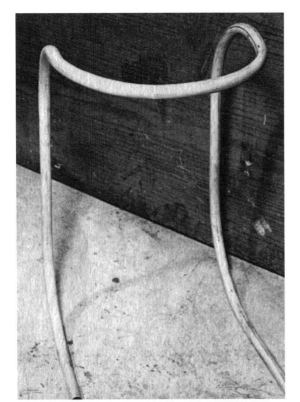

Frame is bent, ready to be cut off.

Although straight pieces of tubing could be used for the sides, they wouldn't conform to the shape of your back and would eventually make the pack hard to carry. To bend the tubing, use an electrician's conduit bender, or fill the tubing with sand, plug both ends with a wooden plug, and bend around a large round object such as a metal barrel. The sand in the tubing prevents it from buckling or crimping at the ends.

Cut the back braces leaving about 1 inch extra length on each end and bend them to shape in the same manner as the side pieces. With the back braces bent to shape, flatten their ends down so they will fit evenly over the side pieces. The initial shaping can be done over a steel rod; however, the final shaping, with light blows, can be done on the tubing to make sure they fit together properly. Using a metal grinder or rasp, round the ends a bit and smooth them down. Place the back braces in position, bore through the crosspiece, down through the first wall of the tubing and use pop rivets to fasten the pieces together. Polish the frame with fine steel wool and use wooden plugs in the end to seal them off.

Ends of braces are peened over a round steel pipe.

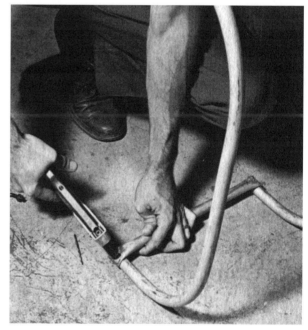

Holes are drilled in braces and frame and braces are pop riveted in place.

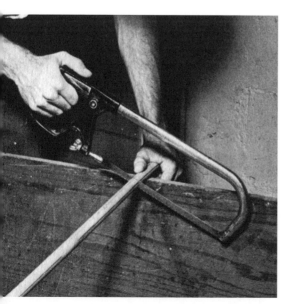

Measure for braces and cut off with hacksaw.

Making the Pack Bag

Traditionally, pack bags were made from canvas, but a better choice would be heavy-duty ripstop nylon such as used for tent floors.

Make the pattern full size and transfer it to the material, then cut the material to the proper shapes and size. Sew the pockets on the sides and front pieces using a double-stitched seam. A good zipper can be made from Velcro, or the pockets can be fastened with snaps or tie strings. The choice is up to you.

Sew the bag together, inside out, using a double-stitched seam for strength. Note that the top of the bag is covered by a heavy-duty flap that is tied down to metal rings (from drapery rods) on the bottom of the pack. These plus the tie loops to tie the pack to the frame must be sewn in between the side, front, and back pieces during the sewing operation.

The straps are made from 2-inch-wide webbing material. Sew them to shoulder pads made by covering 1-inch foam pads with the nylon material. The bottoms of the straps are

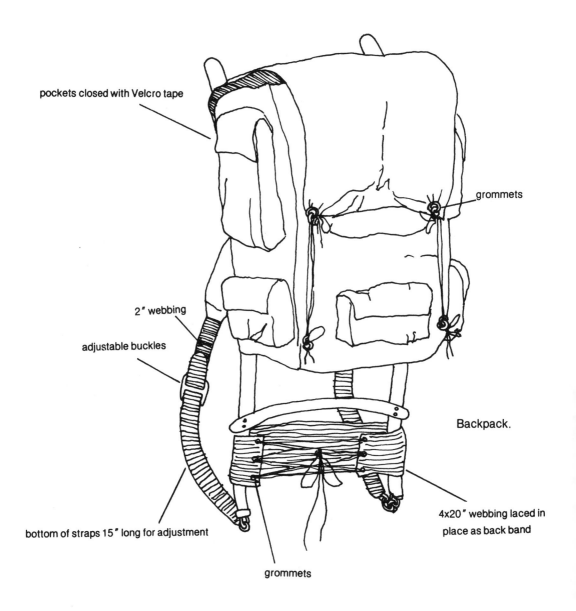

pockets closed with Velcro tape

grommets

2″ webbing

adjustable buckles

Backpack.

bottom of straps 15″ long for adjustment

grommets

4x20″ webbing laced in place as back band

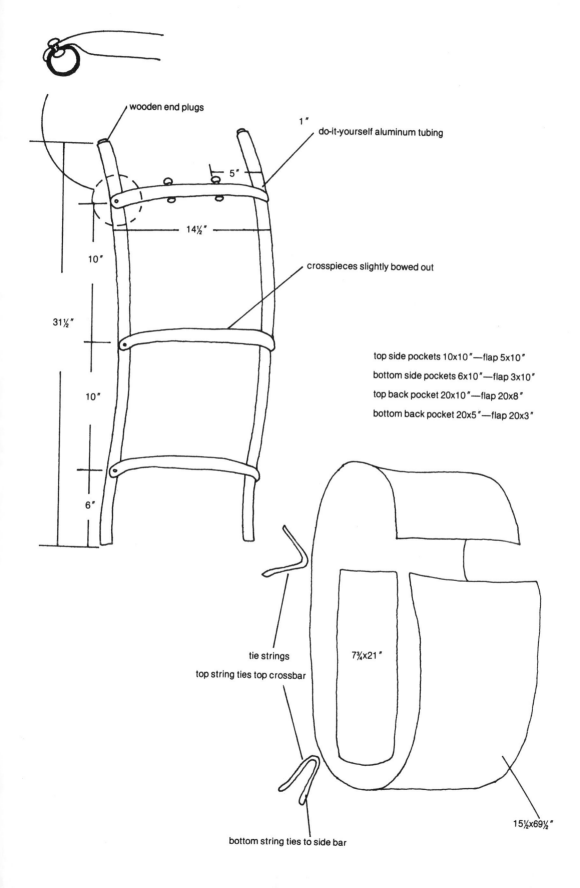

wooden end plugs

1″

do-it-yourself aluminum tubing

5″

14½″

crosspieces slightly bowed out

10″

31½″

10″

6″

top side pockets 10x10″—flap 5x10″

bottom side pockets 6x10″—flap 3x10″

top back pocket 20x10″—flap 20x8″

bottom back pocket 20x5″—flap 20x3″

tie strings

top string ties top crossbar

7¾x21″

15½x69½″

bottom string ties to side bar

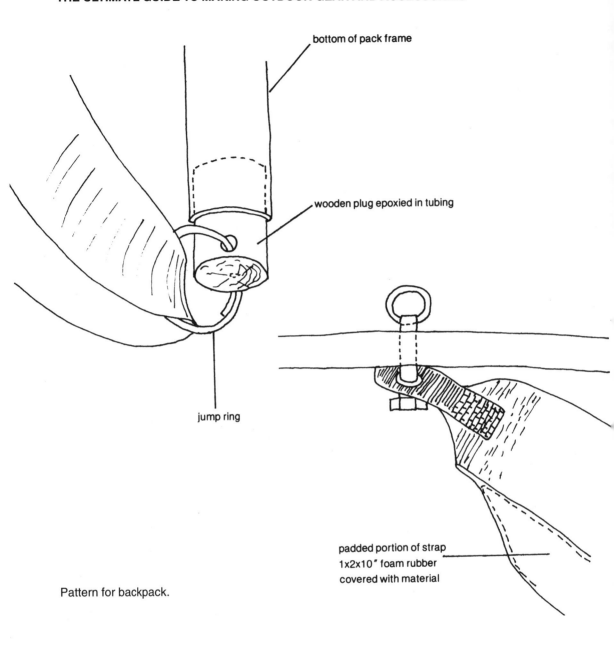

bottom of pack frame

wooden plug epoxied in tubing

jump ring

padded portion of strap
1x2x10″ foam rubber
covered with material

Pattern for backpack.

fitted with adjusting buckles to enable them to be adjusted.

A 4-inch band of double-layer material is placed directly at the bottom as a waistband and is laced onto the pack frame as shown.

On the backpack shown, the sleeping bag is secured at the bottom by loops through holes bored in the bottoms of the side pieces. If you prefer to locate the sleeping bag at the top,

shift the pack to the bottom and make the bag holes in the top of the frame. One of the greatest things about making your own pack frames is that you can make as many different size pockets as you wish on the pack and size them according to what you need them for. In my opinion you can't get enough pockets in a backpack—that is, until you try to find something.

SAWBUCK PACK SADDLES

If you do horseback packing a good pack saddle can save you a lot of work and frustration. Make the saddle from a lightweight wood such as spruce or fine-grained white pine. You will also need some harness leather, buckles, and rivets. The inside edges should be shaped and all edges rounded to prevent them from cutting into the sides of the horse. The wooden parts are held together with waterproof glue, bolts, and nuts.

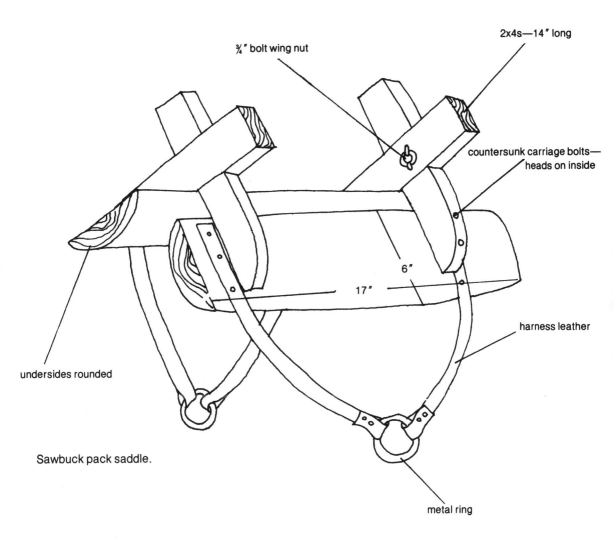

¾" bolt wing nut

2x4s—14" long

countersunk carriage bolts—
heads on inside

6"

17"

harness leather

undersides rounded

metal ring

Sawbuck pack saddle.

13

Moccasins and Other Leather Crafting

Ever since the first caveman learned that an animal skin would keep him warm and protect him from the elements, we have been using animal skins for decoration and protection. Making your own moccasins, belts, shirts, jackets, and vests out of leather can be a most enjoyable hobby.

BASIC LEATHER WORKING

Because each individual item must be sized to fit you, you will have to make your own pattern. Follow the steps shown for the various projects to make a pattern to suit your size. Draw the pattern on heavyweight paper, then transfer it to the leather using a felt-tip pen. Cut on the outlines using a craft razor or other sharp knife. Carefully follow the outlines to ensure that the pattern will fit. The sewing holes may be marked with a small awl made from a piece of wooden dowel with a sharpened nail driven in one end, then ground sharp. The item can be stitched with ⅛-inch rawhide or thin leather-lacing material, or you may wish to stitch the leather together using a waxed thread and

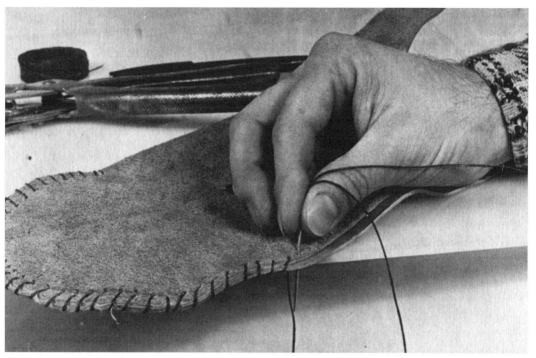

Leather can be stitched with waxed thread and a needle . . .

Or laced.

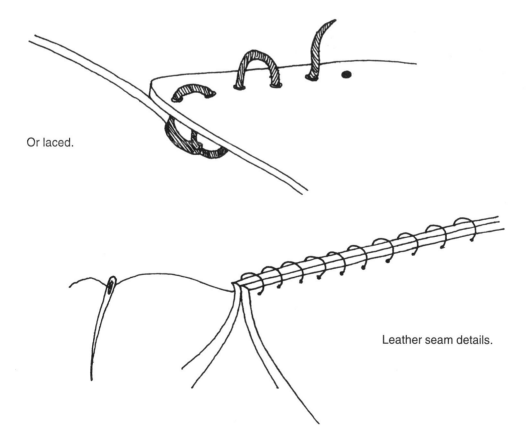

Leather seam details.

needle. Again the holes will have to be punched with a small awl. Make sure all lacing or stitching is even and tightly formed, yet not pulled so tight in some areas to pucker the leather unevenly.

BASIC MOCCASIN PATTERN

This is the easiest moccasin to make. However, it's not as form fitting as other moccasins and has a tendency to be somewhat wide. Since the moccasin is sewn wrong side out, make sure you sew the seams evenly. The moccasin can be made from tanned buckskin or suede leather.

Fold over a piece of heavy paper for a pattern, large enough to place your foot on. Put your foot on the paper with the side of the ball of your foot ½ inch away from the folded side of the paper. Then trace completely around your foot with a felt-tip pen, holding the pen against the foot and straight up and

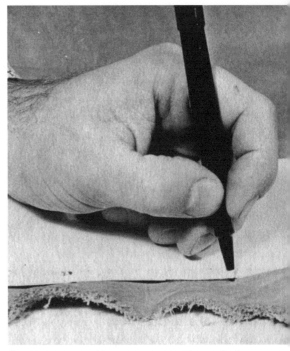

Cut pattern out of heavy paper and transfer it to the leather.

Trace around your foot to make up the pattern, following instructions for individual moccasins.

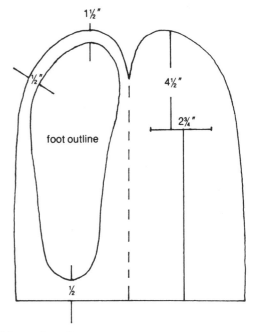

Moccasin pattern.

down. Remove your foot and make a pattern from the drawing. The pattern is drawn ½ inch larger all around than the tracing of your foot. Trace the tongue and flap cuts on the top portion of the moccasin pattern. Cut the pattern to the proper shape and size and place it on a piece of leather. Remember which side of the leather you wish to use for the outside of the moccasins. Trace the pattern onto the leather with a felt-tip pen. Use a sharp razor or craft knife to cut the leather, following the pattern.

Fold over the two halves just like the paper pattern (with moccasin wrong side out), and sew or lace them together starting at the toe of the moccasin. Lace back to within an inch of the end, then temporarily tie off the thread or lacing. Turn the moccasin right side out and place it over your foot. Gather the back material together, and mark for removal of the excess. Also mark at line A to cut in on both sides of the moccasin. This will make the heel of the moccasin. Cut off the pieces and turn the moccasin wrong side out again. Untie the lacing or thread and continue the stitching, completing the back. Tie off the thread or lacing and lace or sew the tongue to

Cut out leather using a razor or craft knife.

the moccasin. Turn it right side out, cut the holes for the lacing if desired, and thread with thongs made from the same material as the moccasins.

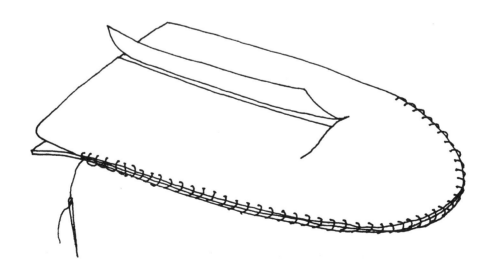

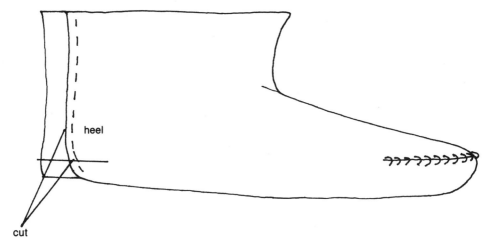

Drawing turned around measuring heel.

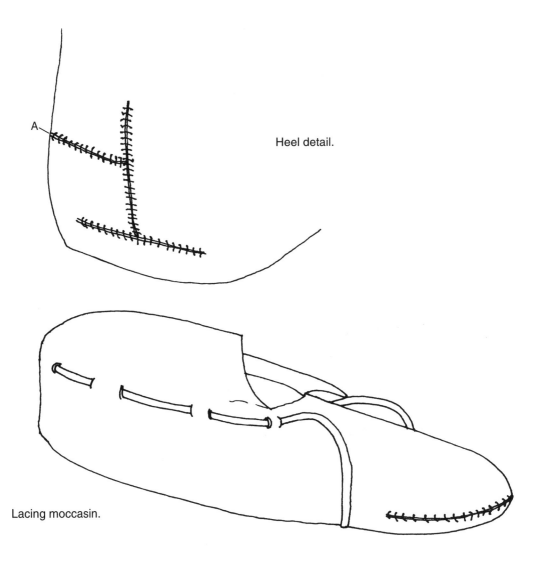

Heel detail.

Lacing moccasin.

One-piece, side-seam moccasin is one of the easiest to make.

Make the other moccasin in the same manner, remembering to turn the pattern over exactly to duplicate the opposite foot pattern.

The moccasins can be decorated with beadwork if you wish to go all out.

CENTER-SEAM MOCCASINS

These moccasins are made from one piece of leather. They look best stitched tightly with waxed thread from the inside out.

Another simple moccasin pattern. It also uses one piece of leather. The seam runs up the back and across the top of the foot.

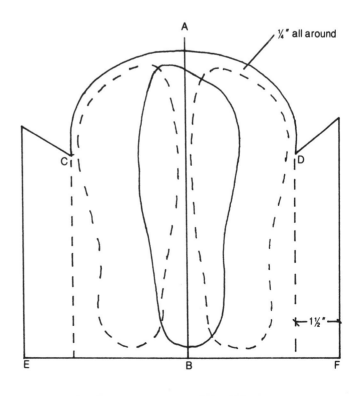

First draw a straight line down the length of a piece of paper. Position your foot over the center of the line with the line running from your toes to your heel, then mark around the outline of your foot. Add ¼ inch to the measurement and mark the measurements A and B as shown. Using a piece of string measure around your foot at the ball of your foot, up near the toes. Use this to mark the measurement C and D. Now move your foot on each. By using the three-foot patterns you will know exactly how much leather you will need to cover your foot. Using the four points as a reference, make the pattern as shown. The side flaps are approximately 1½ inches wide.

Cut the leather to the right shape and size and stitch together tightly. Remember, this moccasin will also be sewn together wrong side out, starting with the toe and running to the heel. Stitch up the back sewing from E-F to B.

PURCHASED PATTERNS

The hardest part of making moccasins is making a pattern that will fit properly. This can be simplified by purchasing presized patterns. These are much like patterns used for sewing other garments, and are available in many different sizes. Trace the patterns off onto the leather, and use the instructions furnished with the pattern for that particular type of boot. The Apache boot shown was taken from a Tandy pattern, except the top was lowered about 3 inches.

KIT-BUILT MOCCASINS

Kits of precut leather moccasins can also be purchased. All you do is lace the pieces together. This is a great way of getting kids started in leatherwork.

MAKING BELTS

Belts are easy to make. You will need punches for cutting the buckle and rivet holes, and a rivet setting tool. The belts can be made in hundreds of ways using precut

This moccasin was made from a purchased, sized pattern. The top has been cut down about 4 inches, modifying the moccasin to suit.

Or you can purchase a kit and merely sew the pieces together.

Making belts is easy. You can purchase precut blanks or cut your own, decorate, and fasten buckle to belt.

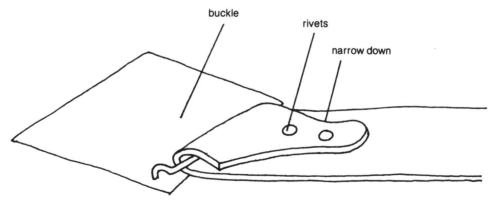

buckle   rivets   narrow down

Belt detail.

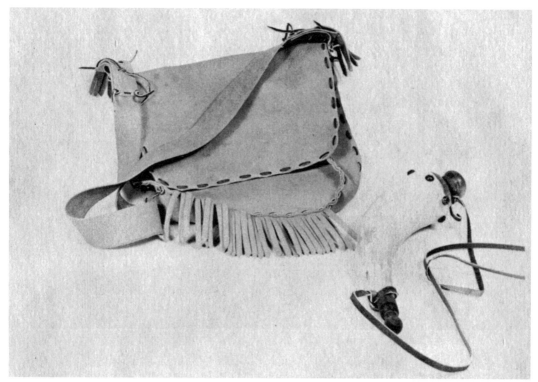

A great addition to your muzzle-loading equipment is this shooter's bag, used for holding powder measurers, starting block, extra patches, etc.

blanks, or you can cut the blanks to size yourself from split cowhide. They may be plain, tooled, or merely stained bright colors. There are literally thousands of belt buckle designs. The buckles are held on in numerous ways, but the most popular is shown.

BLACK POWDER SHOOTER'S BAG

If you've made the powder horn, muzzle-loader, etc., you will probably want to make this shooter's bag. It should be made of suede or some other soft leather. Enlarge the squared drawing onto a piece of heavy paper and make the patterns, then cut the leather pieces to size. Sew the bag together wrong side out or lace it with ⅛-inch leather lacing.

Fasten the carrying strap with thongs through the side pieces.

14

Deer Hunting Stands and Houses

LADDER DEER STAND

The ladder stand shown is comfortable enough to allow you to spend all day in the deer woods. Yet, the deer stand can be carried to a hunting site in a pickup, a tractor or utility vehicle and cart, or even by a couple of hunters. Although I have lifted these stands in place by myself, a helper would definitely be in order because the stand is top heavy until you get it propped in place. After that, it's a matter of tying the stand to the tree with nylon rope, or wiring it in place if you prefer. Wire can cause damage to the tree unless a piece of rubber hose is slipped over the wire before installing. I also use a secondary tie rope, tied to the second from the bottom rung, run around the tree and then tied to the opposite ladder side to hold the bottom of the stand solidly in place. For safety, I tie this rope securely in place before climbing up the ladder to secure the top rope. It also is a very good idea to have someone on hand to hold the stand until you can get it securely attached to the tree. When erecting the stand make sure it is positioned level and on solid,

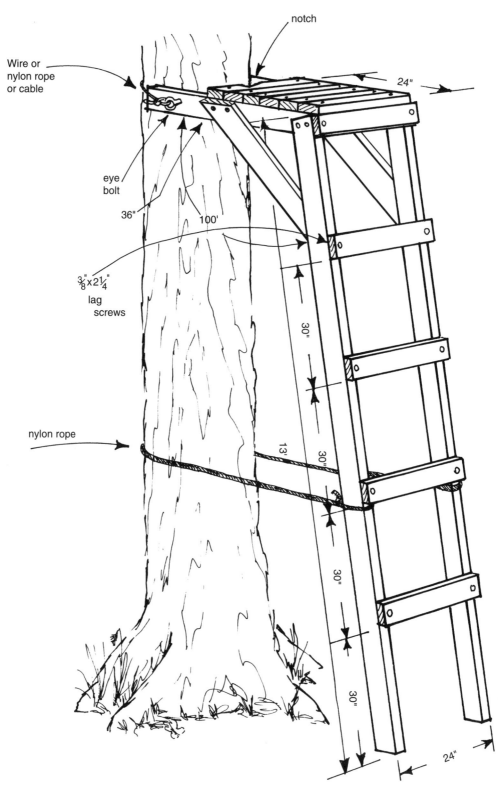

Deer stand.

smooth ground, and there are no obstacles such as rocks or roots that can cause the stand to tip or turn sideways. The notch in the back of each of the side support boards of the seat helps keep the stand from sliding sideways, but it is extremely important that the top of the stand be tied securely in place.

Caution: Always use a safety harness while using any treestand.

The stand is made from standard 2 × 4 treated lumber and you will need a total of two 16-foot, one 12-foot and one 10-foot 2 × 4s for each stand. Make sure the 2 × 4s are all solid and the ends cut square because all of the lumber will be used for the stand. The stand can be painted in a camouflage pattern to match the surrounding area or it can be left to weather naturally.

Construction

Construction is simple, several of the stands can be built in a single afternoon. The first step is to cut three feet from the end of each of the 16-foot boards to make the two seat side supports and two ladder sides. Then cut the 12-foot 2 × 4 into the 6 seat top pieces and cut the 10-foot 2 × 4 into the 5 ladder steps.

Fasten the steps to the ladder sides using $3/8 × 3$ inch lag bolts. Note that the top step is left off until the seat portion is in place. Fasten the seat boards to the seat supports with 2½ inch self-starting deck screws, making sure to overhang the seat boards 1½ inches on each side as the ladder sides will be fitted outside the seat supports. Then fasten the seat support ends inside the ladder sides at a 100-degree angle as shown using $3/8 × 3$ inch lag bolts. Position the top step in place directly under the front seat board and fasten it in place with the self-starting deck screws. Attach the two eye bolts on the back end of the seat supports and cut a one-inch deep notch in the back end of the seat side supports for the rope or

wire. Use rope or wire to attach the stand to a tree. Small hooks could be added to the outside of the seat supports to hang binoculars, rattling antlers, and other gear or bags. A camouflage cushion will also add to the comfort of your stand.

Materials List
A. Ladder Sides; 2 x 4 x 13', 2 reqd.
B. Ladder Steps; 2 x 4 x 24", 5 reqd.
C. Seat Supports; 2 x 4 x 36", 2 reqd.
D. Seat Top; 2 x 4 x 24", 6 reqd.
E. Braces, 2 x 4 x 24", cut to fit, 2 reqd.
F. Eye bolts.
Lag bolts; $3/8 × 3$", 14 reqd.
Deck screws

SHOOTING HOUSE

Shooting houses placed over feed fields, food plots, and major trails offer a lot of advantages. The first, of course, is the comfort. Shooting houses also conceal movement and cut down on scent as well. The house shown is a basic design that can be positioned as a permanent house on the ground, or positioned up on a platform. It can also be fitted with 4 × 4 skids and pulled to various locations with an ATV, making it even more portable. The house is constructed of economical precut studs ripping some in half to create the 1½-inch thick materials. The exterior is pressure treated ½-inch plywood for durability. Exterior plywood can also be used. The windows are simple lift-up flaps. Sliding aluminum storm windows can be substituted and not only offer more comfort, but also help hold in scent better.

Construction

First step is to cut the front side supports, front bottom and top supports, shelf support, and front to the correct size. The supports are first ripped from 2 × 4 material using a ripping guide and a portable electric saw, or

Shooting house provides enclosed comfort and helps prevent spooking game with movement or scent.

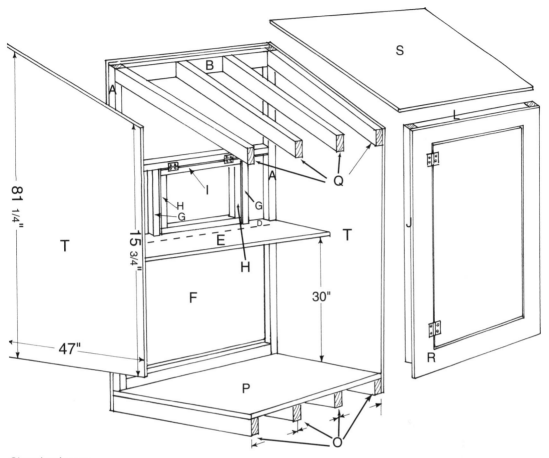

Shooting house.

table or radial arm saw. Lay the front side supports on a smooth flat surface with the top and bottom front supports between them. Fasten together with 2 1/2-inch self-starting wood screws driven through the side supports into the ends of the top and bottom supports. Make sure the front framework is square, then place the front down on top of it and install with 1 1/4-inch self-starting wood screws. Note the lower portion of the front extends below the front bottom piece so it can be fastened to the bottom framework.

Cut and assemble the back framework in the same manner. Note the back door supports extend to the top edge of the back support and must be notched to fit around the

back supports. Once the framework is assembled, install the back.

Cut the bottom floor joists to size. Cut the bottom, lay the joists on a smooth flat surface and fasten the floor on the joists with 2 1/2-inch self-starting wood screws.

With the floor assembly completed, position the front assembly in place with the lower portion of the front overlapping the front of the floor assembly and the front bottom piece resting on the floor. Use a square to assure it is positioned square, then fasten in place with 2 1/2-inch self-starting wood screws down through the front bottom piece into the bottom assembly, and through the lower front into the ends of the floor joists.

Position the rear assembly in place and fasten in the same manner. Then fasten the two sides to the front and back. Cut the door in the back. A portable circular saw can first be used to make "pocket starting cuts," by holding the saw away from the material, starting it and slowly allowing the blade to cut through until the cut is started. Then continue the cut. A handsaw is used to make the final cuts at the corners. The cut-out door can simply be hinged in place, but it's best to add stiffeners on all sides. These are $1\frac{1}{2} \times 1\frac{1}{2}$-inch pieces cut to fit between the back top support and back door supports. Position them on the insides of the door opening and fasten in place with $1\frac{1}{4}$-inch self-starting screws through the back into the stiffeners. Hinge the door and add a screen door fastener on both the inside and the outside to fasten. You may also wish to cut a peephole in the door.

Cut the top rafters to the proper length, cutting their ends to the correct angles as shown. Fasten the rafters in place between the front and back top pieces with $2\frac{1}{2}$-inch self-starting wood screws. Cut the top to the correct size and fasten it down in place with $1\frac{1}{4}$-inch self-starting wood screws.

Cutting the window requires some special steps. The first step is to place a comfortable chair or stool, one that you intend to use for seating in the house. Sit in the chair or on the stool and determine where you want the window located. The measurement shown is for a standard folding chair and standard table height. Once you have determined the height for the window, mark the location from the inside on the front. Use a square and straightedge to make the outline. Cut out the window in the same manner as the door. After the opening is made add stiffeners to the inside edges, hinge and add screen door hooks, one to hold the window closed and one to hold it open. Install the shelf support and position the shelf just under the front window. You may wish to add windows to the sides as well.

Paint the blind in a camouflage pattern. Use a medium brown latex paint to provide a base coat. Use spray cans of paint to spray a black and dark green leaf pattern over the base coat.

Materials List
A. Front side supports; $1\frac{1}{2} \times 1\frac{1}{2} \times 77\frac{1}{2}$, 2 reqd.
B. Front top support; 2 x 4 x 45", 1 reqd.
C. Front bottom support; $1\frac{1}{2} \times 1\frac{1}{2} \times 45$, 1 reqd.
D. Front shelf and window support; $1\frac{1}{2} \times 1\frac{1}{2} \times 45$", 2 reqd.
E. Shelf; $\frac{3}{4} \times 24 \times 48$", 1 reqd.
F. Front; $\frac{1}{2}$" plywood, 48 x $81\frac{1}{4}$, 1 reqd.
G. Front window supports; $1\frac{1}{2} \times 1\frac{1}{2} \times 12$", 2 reqd
H. Front window verticals; $1\frac{1}{2} \times 1\frac{1}{2} \times 9$", 2 reqd
I. Front window horizontals; $1\frac{1}{2} \times 1\frac{1}{2} \times 24$", 2 reqd.
J. Back side supports; $1\frac{1}{2} \times 1\frac{1}{2} \times 72$", 2 reqd.
K. Back door supports; $1\frac{1}{2} \times 3\frac{1}{2} \times 72$", notched to fit, 2 reqd.
L. Back top support; $1\frac{1}{2} \times 3\frac{1}{2} \times 45$", 1 reqd.
M. Back door verticals; $1\frac{1}{2} \times 1\frac{1}{2} \times 68$", 2 reqd.
N. Back door horizontals; $1\frac{1}{2} \times 1\frac{1}{2} \times 33$", 2 reqd.
O. Bottom floor joists; 2 x 4, 4 reqd.
P. Bottom; $\frac{3}{4}$" plywood; 47 x 48", 1 reqd.
Q. Rafters; $1\frac{1}{2} \times 3\frac{1}{2} \times 45$", cut to fit, 4 reqd.
R. Back; $\frac{1}{2}$" plywood, 48 x $76\frac{1}{4}$", 1 reqd.
S. Top; $\frac{1}{2}$" plywood, 48 x 48", 1 reqd.
T. Sides; $\frac{1}{2}$" plywood, 47 x $81\frac{1}{4}$", 2 reqd.
Fasteners
Self-starting wood screws; No 6 x $1\frac{1}{4}$" long, 8 dozen reqd.
Self-starting wood screws; No 8 x $2\frac{1}{2}$", 6 dozen reqd.
Butt hinges; $1\frac{1}{2}$", 1 pair reqd.
Butt hinges; 3", 1 pair reqd.
Screen door hooks; 4 reqd.
Green, brown, and black camouflage paint.

15

Miscellaneous

TRAINING DUMMYS

A dog can be trained to retrieve with a stick or a stuffed sock, but a proper training dummy is easier to throw and gives the dog a special item he knows he must retrieve. Make it out of a 12 × 16 piece of canvas. Sew it together as shown, wrong side out, and stuff it with old socks or rags, then sew the end shut. Double the end over twice and sew completely around it. Install a grommet in the end.

CHECK CORDS

When training young dogs in the field, you'll need a check cord to halt them at the proper time. Make one from a 25-foot length of nylon rope, a snap swivel, and a choke collar. Make a loop in one end of the rope for your hand, fastening the loop with a whipped end. Then make another loop in the opposite end and fasten it around the snap swivel before adding the choke collar.

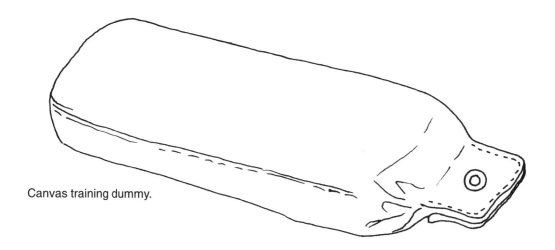

Canvas training dummy.

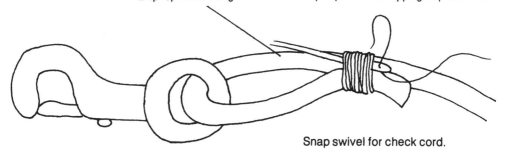

monofilament loop

whip rope ends using monofilament loop to pull loose whipping loop back under itself

Snap swivel for check cord.

QUAIL CALL BOXES

Using live, pen-raised birds not only speeds up the training of a young dog, but it can help revitalize an old dog as well. The quail call box shown helps to eliminate the common problem of quail escaping in the field. Quail are naturally gregarious and they will call their group or family back together. What is needed is a box divided down the middle, with an opening on one side. The quail are taken out of one side and used for dog training, then the box with the remaining quail is placed in the field and left for a while. The birds that remain in the box will call the others that are in the field back to the box. The birds enter through the funnel-shaped opening but can't get back out again.

Make the box with 2 × 2 framing and cover with ¼-inch mesh hardware cloth.

DOG KENNELS

Homes for dogs can be almost anything from a sack in the corner of the garage to a rug by the fireplace. However, most hunting dogs do best if they are kept conditioned to the outside weather. This doesn't mean freezing the dog to death in poor housing, but rather giving it a snug warm house and an enclosed run.

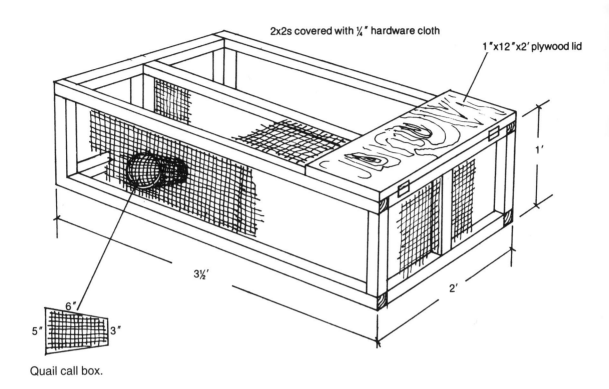

2x2s covered with ¼" hardware cloth

1"x12"x2' plywood lid

1'

3½'

2'

6"

5"   3"

Quail call box.

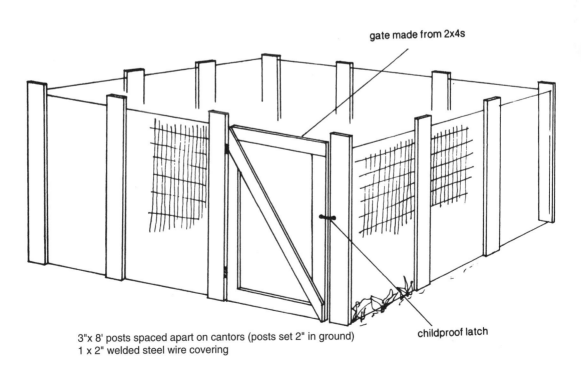

gate made from 2x4s

childproof latch

3"x 8' posts spaced apart on cantors (posts set 2" in ground)
1 x 2" welded steel wire covering

Dog kennel.

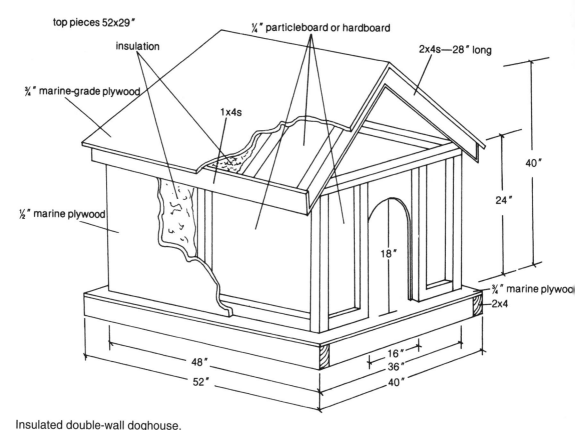

Insulated double-wall doghouse.

The kennel can be made from prepackaged metal fencing or steel-welded wire and wooden posts. The top of the kennel should have a slanted portion or the kennel should be 6 feet high, especially if you have female dogs. Make the floor of concrete with a slight slope at one end so it can be cleaned properly with a garden hose.

The house should be snug and warm. The house shown is an insulated double-wall house. The sides and ends are assembled backwards by nailing the inside plywood pieces to a 2 × 2 frame. Then these pieces are fastened together, insulation installed, and the outside plywood pieces nailed in place. The top and bottom are made in the same manner.

Paint the doghouse with a latex house paint, and seal the peak at the roof with caulking compound.

SWIMMING DOCKS

The small swimming dock shown will greatly increase the fun and enjoyment of a backyard pond or lake. Use 9-foot preformed sections of foam plastic flotation to make the dock. Three pieces are used for the flotation. All pieces should be precut and all holes bored at home then carted down to the pond, and the dock assembled at the water's edge. The first step is to cut the four side pieces, and assemble them using lag bolts. Place the three flotation pieces inside this frame and set the frame up

Completed swimming dock.

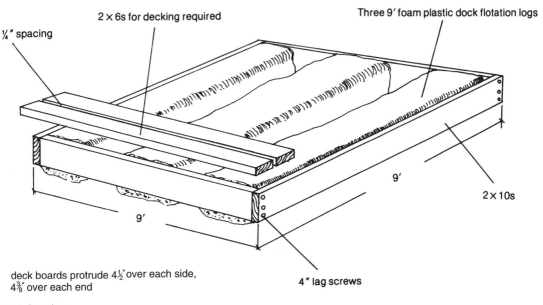

2 × 6s for decking required

¼″ spacing

Three 9′ foam plastic dock flotation logs

9′

2 × 10s

9′

deck boards protrude 4½″ over each side,
4⅜″ over each end

4″ lag screws

Deck framing.

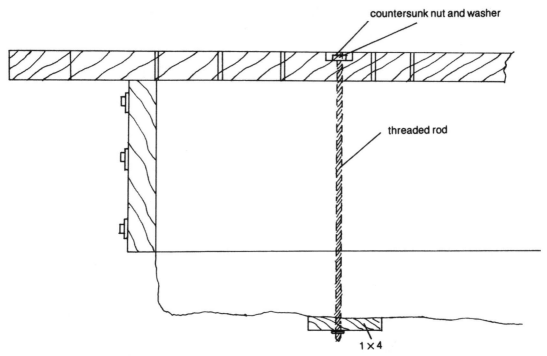

Fastening flotation to deck.

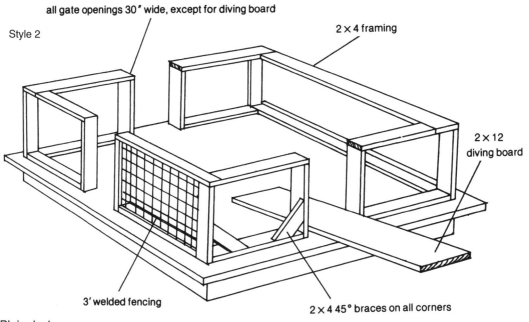

Plain deck.

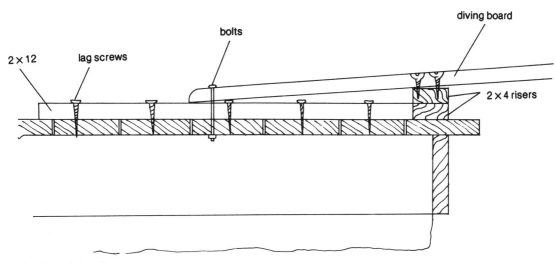

Diving board details.

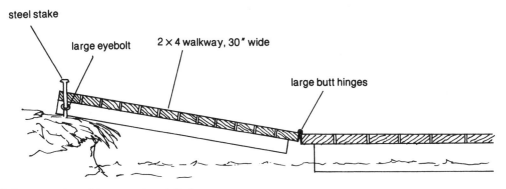

Walkway anchored to ground and dock.

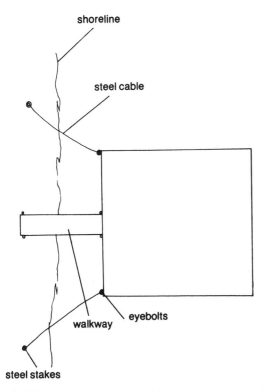

Anchoring dock.

on wood blocks to raise the outside edge above the flotation frame. Nail the precut 2 × 6 decking pieces in place on the top edge of the outside frame using a piece of ¼-inch plywood between them as a spacer. Use galvanized nails or deck screws for all fastening. Keep the ends of the decking even, and make sure the frame is square before you fasten the decking pieces down securely.

With the decking on, cut the railing and post pieces and assemble them on the docks, then fasten welded steel wire in place. The diving board is an option; the dock is so small that it will rock somewhat when the diving board is used. Wire-covered gates would also be a good idea for docks that are to be used by small children. Install hardware, tie the dock off to land, and push it into the water.

DO-IT-YOURSELF BUOYS

Buoys for marking fishing areas or to locate a scuba diving area can be made easily and economically from a couple of Styro-foam balls, a piece of wooden dowel, fishing line, and a weight. The foam balls can be any size, depending on the type of water conditions you experience. Bore a hole in the foam balls and pour ordinary white glue in them.

Cut a 1-inch wooden dowel to 5 inches and insert it in the holes. Turn the dowel back and forth in the holes to get it well coated with the glue, then allow to set overnight until the glue sets up. Dip or brush the foam balls with latex house paint as a sealing coat, then tape off the handle and half of the balls and spray with bright orange paint.

Tie monofilament fishing line to the handle and wrap it around the handle, then fasten it to a weight such as an anchor weight. Secure the line and anchor to the handle with a large rubber band.

To use the buoy, remove the rubber band holding the line and anchor, and merely pitch the buoy in the water. It will automatically unwind until the weight reaches the bottom marking the spot quickly and easily.

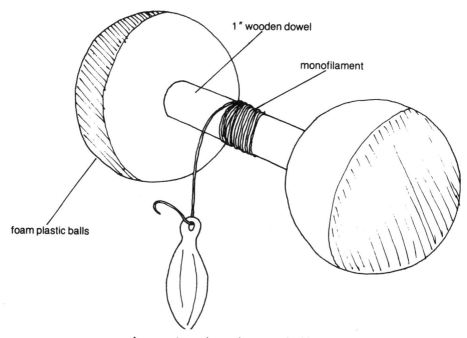

An easy-to-make and economical buoy.

BOAT SEAT PEDESTALS

A throne pedestal seat for small johnboats can be made using two pieces of wood, a piece of heavy-gauge sheet metal, and a purchased plastic swivel chair.

Cut the wooden pieces to size. Use a squared edge such as a workbench top to bend the metal piece into the right shape. Bore holes in the top and sides for the wood screws and fasten the metal shell to the wooden sides, with round-head screws. Position the pedestal in place on the deck and bore holes for the holding bolts. Bolt the pedestal in position.

Place the chair and pedestal over the seat in the boat and mark for bolt hole locations. Clamp the pedestal in place while boring through the chair flange and the seat flange at the same time. When all holes have been bored, remove the pedestal and place a doubled-over section of old inner tube between it and the boat as a "gasket," then bolt securely in place.

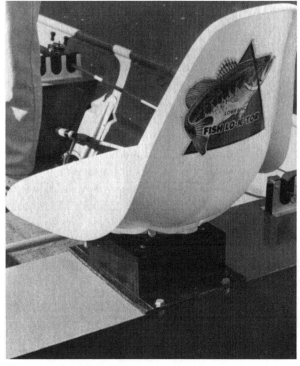

Throne pedestal chair.

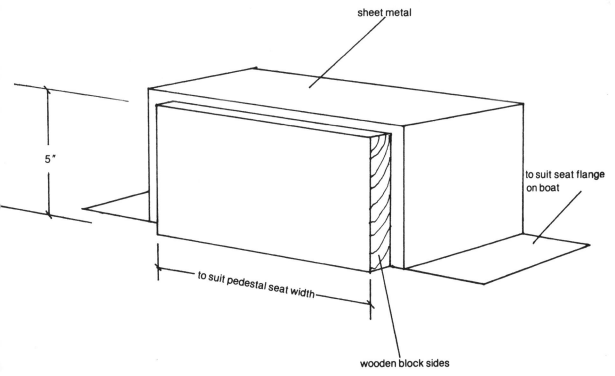

Pattern for throne pedestal chair.

BOAT DECKS

A deck on small johnboats can be a help, and if using a front-operated trolling motor they're a necessity. The johnboat shown here was made much more effective by the use of a front-deck and front-operating electric trolling motor. Measure for the size of the deck and cut it from a piece of ¾-inch marine-grade plywood. Coat all surfaces of the wood with good protective paint or a marine varnish. Place it in position on the gunwales and clamp securely. Bore holes through both the plywood and the gunwales, then secure with bolts and nuts. Place the trolling motor in place and secure it with bolts. Note the two screw eyes on the side to thread the anchor through, which makes for neat and easy anchoring.

SLINGSHOTS

Slingshots can be great for plinking and target shooting or hunting small animals. The one shown is made of ¾-inch hardwood stock and is decorated by checkering the

A plywood deck for small johnboats, as shown in photo, is easy to make.

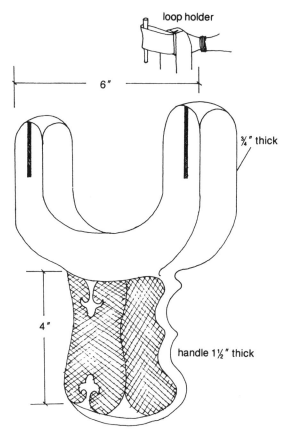

loop holder

6″

¾″ thick

4″

handle 1½″ thick

Pattern for slingshot.

stock or grip. The grip portion is built to the proper thickness by gluing two pieces of stock together. First cut out the basic shape on a band saw, etc., then glue the second piece to the handle. Round all edges and shape the handle with a rasp. Smooth with progressively finer grits of sandpaper, and finish with a spray gunstock finish, or wipe with gunstock finishing oil. Rubber surgical tubing may be used for the sling, or you can cut it from an old inner tube. It is threaded through a leather pocket and fastened to the frame by running it through the saw slots, turning it around a small wooden dowel, then pulling it back through and whip stitching the two pieces together using monofilament fishing line.

BOOT ANCHORS

One great way of recycling an old pair of waders is to make boat anchors out of them. Merely cut off the bottom parts and pour them full of concrete. Before the concrete sets you can bend over a bolt in a U-shape and embed it in the concrete. Not only are

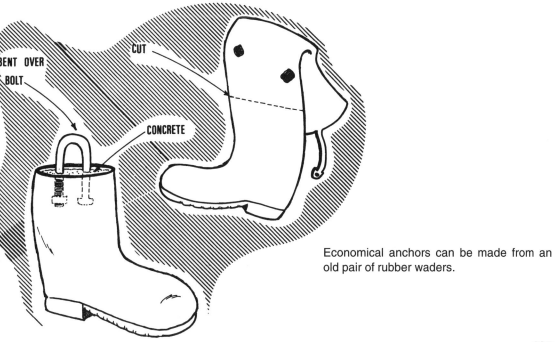

BENT OVER

BOLT

CUT

CONCRETE

Economical anchors can be made from an old pair of rubber waders.

An army ammunition box makes an excellent waterproof camera box.

these anchors the right size for holding small boats in place, but since they are covered with rubber they won't scar up the finish on your boat.

WATERPROOF CAMERA BOXES

One disadvantage of commercially made camera boxes is that most of them aren't entirely waterproof and even worse they look like a camera box, making them a prime target for thieves.

A most effective camera box for those who enjoy water sports can be made from an army ammunition box purchased from an army surplus store. Make sure the box you purchase is watertight by testing it in the bathtub or kitchen sink before using it to store a camera in. Paint the inside of the lid in a reflective color and line the bottom and sides with 1-inch foam rubber. Spray paint the outside in some easy to spot reflective color and fasten a short dog chain to the handle. In the event of a turnover during canoeing, the camera box will be secure and easily seen.

SHOOTING BENCH

The shooting bench shown is actually a portable table you can take in the back of your pickup to the shooting site. Or you can modify it into a permanent bench by using treated 4 × 4s cut two feet longer than the legs in the drawing and permanently setting them in the ground with concrete poured around them. The height allows the use of a folding chair or patio chair.

The bench is constructed of treated 2 × 4 stock with a top of treated plywood so it can withstand being left out in the weather. Don't use untreated wood for the project as it won't last more than one or two seasons. The project is completely assembled with exterior, self-starting (deck) wood screws. This provides a long lasting and sturdy assembly. When used with a powerful cordless screwdriver such as the Craftsman Industrial ½-inch 18.0 volt drill/driver and a Craftsman Speed-Lok Power Driver, assembly is fast and easy. The latter is magnetized and has a slide-down sleeve to hold the screw until it gets started.

Shooting table is easily transported in the back of a pickup and set up for in-the-field sighting in and practice.

Construction

Begin construction by first cutting the legs and side supports to length, making sure all cuts are square. Lay the rear legs on a smooth flat surface. Position the rear top support in place and fasten each end to the top end of the legs with a 2½-inch self-starting screw. Use a carpenter's square to assure the assembly is square and drive a second screw in each end. Place the lower rear support piece in position and fasten it in place with screws. Assemble the front leg assembly in the same manner.

Stand the rear leg and front leg assembly up on one edge and fasten the top left side support in place by first driving one screw in each end, using a carpenter's square to make sure the assembly is square, then driving two more screws in each end. Fasten the bottom left side support in place in the same way. Then stand the assembly up on the left side and fasten the right side supports in place with screws and adding the fifth leg to the right side supports.

Cut the ¾-inch plywood top to the correct size and shape. Use a straightedge and carpenter's square to mark the measurements. The corners are rounded and the radiuses are marked by simply placing a 3-pound coffee can in place and marking around the bottom edge. The rounded corners are cut using a saber saw. Lightly sand all edges of the top to remove any sharp edges.

Stand the leg assembly upright, position the top down on the leg assembly and fasten the top in place using 1½-inch self-starting wood screws.

The table can be left as is, or given a coat of exterior paint or protective deck preservative.

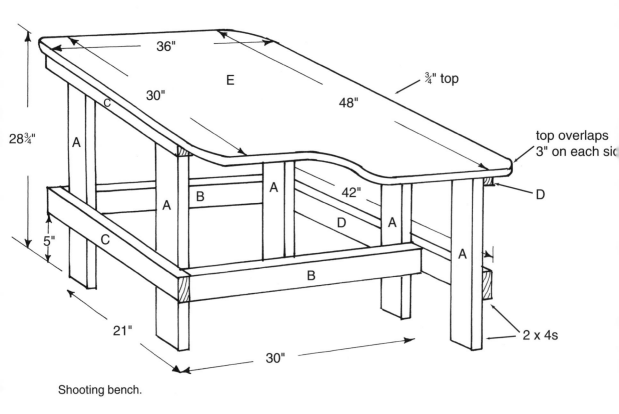

Shooting bench.

Materials List

A. Legs; 2 × 4 × 28", 5 reqd.
B. Front and back leg supports (top and bottom);
   2 × 4 × 28½" , 4 reqd.
C. Left side supports; 2 × 4 × 24", 2 reqd.
D. Right side supports; 2 × 4 × 42", 2 reqd.
E. Top; ¾" plywood, 36 × 48", 1 reqd.
Self-starting wood screws, No. 8 × 2½", 3 dozen
   reqd.
Self-starting wood screws, No. 8 × 1½", 2 dozen
reqd.

BUILD A FISH AND/OR BAIT HOLDING BOX

A live fish or bait box is handy if you need to keep fish until they can be released in another area, or until you decide to dress them for eating. The same box can also be used to hold large numbers of bait such as minnows, goldfish, or crawfish. The box is designed to float in the water and can be attached to a dock or simply fastened to an anchor on the bank.

Because the box is mostly submerged in water, it is made entirely of pressure treated lumber and plywood. Exterior self-starting wood screws and galvanized nails are used to fasten the box together. Galvanized hardware cloth or fiberglass screen wire is used to cover the box, with protective cleats outside and over the wire to provide further strength.

Construction

The framework is made of 2 × 2s (actually 1½ × 1½ inches) ripped from a pressure treated 2 × 6. The boards can be ripped to width using a table saw, radial arm saw, or portable circular saw with a ripping fence. The framework pieces are then cut to length, with two long pieces and two short pieces for

Floating fish box can be used to hold fish for dressing, or to keep fish until they can be released into another area.

The floating box can also be used to hold bait such as minnows, goldfish, or crawfish.

Box is assembled from pressure treated wood using exterior wood screws.

The opening in the top for the door is made using a portable circular saw to create pocket cuts.

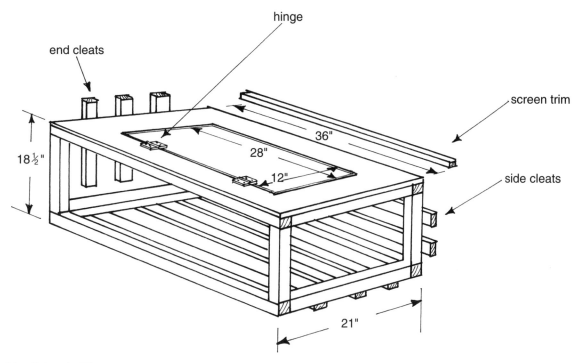

Live fish or bait box.

both top and bottom framework and four uprights.

Fasten the top framework together using 2¼-inch self-starting, exterior wood screws. In order to prevent the ends splitting as the screws are driven, pre-drill all screw holes first with a ⅛-inch bit. To begin construction position a long piece over two short pieces of the top framework and drive the screws tightly in place. Position the opposite long piece over the ends of the two short pieces and fasten it in place. Repeat for the opposite or bottom framework. Then, with the bottom and top framework assembled, fasten the short upright sections between the two frameworks in the same manner, pre-drilling for the screws and fastening with the self-starting wood screws.

The top is cut from a piece of ½-inch pressure treated plywood, using a portable circular saw. The Accu Rip, available from Craftsman, makes cutting the piece from a full sheet of plywood quite easy. Simply attach the Accu Rip to the portable circular saw, set the distance to be cut and follow the edge of the plywood with the guide. The Accu Rip guide can be removed from the saw within seconds.

Fasten the top in place down over the top framework with the 1¼-inch self-starting exterior wood screws. Mark the outline of the door in the top and, using a portable circular saw, cut out the door by making a pocket cut. To begin, hold the front of the saw down securely on the board with the saw blade not touching but in line with the cut. Pull back the blade guard with one finger and start the saw, then slowly lower the blade into the wood until the blade is running freely. Cut up almost to the corner of the cut with the saw blade. Make all four opening cuts in the same manner. The remaining material at the corners can then be cut away with a handsaw or saber saw.

The box must have some sort of flotation materials to keep it afloat. Pieces of packing Styrofoam, or dock Styrofoam can be used. I used an old swimming pool "fun-noodle" that my grandkids had discarded, cutting it into two pieces and placing one on each side, inside and under the plywood top. The foam pieces, or flotation, are held in place with screws with large flat washers on them.

The next step is to install the wire covering. Hardware cloth can be used if you don't plan to use the box for bait. If the box is to be used for holding small baits such as minnows, you may prefer to use screen wire. Fiberglass screen wire works quite well and doesn't rust. To install, cut the pieces to fit each side, end, or bottom. Temporarily fasten the screen wire in place with staples. Then rip ¾-inch thick strips from ¾-inch material and tack them down over the wire edges with galvanized nails or 1¼-inch exterior self-starting wood screws. Place these strips along all edges to permanently hold the wire in place.

Bottom and side cleats, cut from ¾-inch material, offer more strength to the box, not only for holding large fish, but to prevent turtles from getting to the fish, a common problem where these fish eaters exist. Cut the cleats to length and fasten in place with 1¼-inch self-starting exterior wood screws.

Hinge the door in place and add a screen-door hook to keep the lid shut. Raccoons and otters can quickly learn to open a lid without some sort of catch. I've also had catfish bang hard enough on fish boxes to open an unlatched lid and escape.

The final step is to add screw eyes for tying the box to a dock or bank anchor.

Materials List
A. Top and bottom frame pieces; 1½ × 1½ × 36", 4 reqd.
B. Top and bottom frame pieces; 1½ × 1½ × 18", 4 reqd.
C. Vertical frame pieces; 1½ × 1½ × 15", 4 reqd.
D. Top; ½-inch plywood × 21 × 36", 1 reqd.
E. Top screen trim; ¾ × ¾ × 37½", 2 reqd.
F. Top screen trim; ¾ × ¾ × 21", 2 reqd.
G. Bottom screen trim; ¾ × ¾ × 37½", 2 reqd.
H. Corner screen trim; ¾ × ¾ × 21", 8 reqd.
I. End cleats; ¾ × 1½ × 19¼", 6 reqd.
J. Side cleats; ¾ × 1½ × 36", 4 reqd.
K. Bottom cleats; ¾ × 1½ × 36", 3 reqd.
Screen wire or hardware cloth; Cut to fit.
Screws; 2¼" and 1¼", exterior self-starting wood screws.
Nails; No. 4, galvanized
Hinge; 1½" butt hinge, one pair reqd.
Screen door hook; 1 reqd.
Screw eyes; 2 reqd.
Flotation materials.

Materials and Supplies

GUNSMITHING MATERIALS
Brownell's Inc.
641-623-5401
www.brownells.com
www.gunsmithsupply.com

Gun Parts Corporation
845-679-2417
www.e-gunparts.com

GUN STOCKS
Great American Gunstock Co.
800-784-GUNS
www.gunstocks.com

Precision Gun Works
830-367-4587
www.precisiongunstocks.com

Wenig Custom Gunstocks, Inc.
660-547-3334
www.wenig.com

MUZZLELOADING
Connecticut Valley Arms (CVA)
770-449-4687
www.cva.com

Dixie Gun Works, Inc.
800-238-6785
www.dixiegunworks.com

Green Mountain Rifle Barrels
603-447-1095

ARCHERY
3Rivers Archery
260-587-9501
www.3riversarchery.com

Canadian Traditional Archery
780-998-2770
www.traditionalarchery.com

Mystik Longbows
309-785-5109
www.mystiklongbows.com

Silver Arrow Archery
603-434-0569
www.silverarrowarchery.com

DECOY MAKING

Herter's, Inc.
800-654-3825
www.herters.com

KNIFEMAKING

Admiral Steel
800-323-7055
www.admiralsteel.com

Brownell's Inc.
641-623-5401
www.brownells.com,
www.gunsmithsupply.com

Dixie Gun Works, Inc.
800-238-6785
www.dixiegunworks.com

Jantz Supply
800-351-8900
www.knifemaking.com

Kovel Knives
800-556-4837
www.kmg.org/kovelknives

Sheffield Knifemakers Supply
800-874-7007

Texas Knifemakers Supply
713-461-8632

FISHING TACKLE

Barlow's Tackle Shop
972-231-5982
www.barlowtackle.com

Do-It Corp.
319-984-6055
www.do-itmolds.com

Gudebrod, Inc.
610-327-4050
www.gudebrod.com

Jann's Netcraft
800-346-6590
www.jannsnetcraft.com

Last Cast Inc.
732-785-0737
www.customrodbuilders.com

Mud Hole Custom Tackle
800-420-6049
www.mudhole.com

NuWave Tackle
610-718-8837
www.nuwavetackle.com

Shoff Tackle Co.
253-852-4760
www.shofftackle.com

The Worth Co.
715-344-6081
www.worthco.com

Index